BALI

SANGSIT

GARADJA

KARANGASEM

ABANAN
BEDOELOE
BONAH
KLOENGKOENG

DENPASAR

NGESA PENIDA

OCEAN

BALI

BALI

PHILIP HANSON HISS

DUELL, SLOAN AND PEARCE

NEW YORK

FOR MARJORIE

Contents

Illustrations

ILLUSTRATIONS xi

xii   *ILLUSTRATIONS*

GLOSSARY

KEY TO PRONUNCIATION

It has been thought best to spell all Balinese, Malay, or Dutch words in their customary Dutch fashion, with the exception of certain words which are already well known to the public in their Anglicized forms. In Dutch oe is pronounced as oo in food; tj as ch in chime; dj as j; j as y; and g as g in go.

Adat: traditional religious and secular law.

Agoeng: high, great, or most important.

Arak: rice brandy.

Artja: a small wooden figure, either male or female, into which the spirit of the deity enters on special occasions.

Badjoe: a blouse worn by Javanese women and imported into North Bali during the latter part of the nineteenth century.

Balé: a roofed platform.

Bandjar: an independent ward within a desa.

Barong: a mythical lion who uses his great magic power on the side of good.

Batik: a cloth with a design in colors, made by coating the parts not to be dyed with wax.

Bhoma Head: an ornament found over the gateways of most Balinese temples; it is probably identical with the head of the Barong.

Brom: a sherry made from fermented rice.

Dagang: a girl or a woman who sells food or drink from behind a small table which she carries to the scene of any gathering.

Dalang: a storyteller; the man who recites the stories and manipulates the puppets in the shadow play.

Desa: a small communalistic village.

Djeroek: a fruit similar to a grapefruit, though coarser in texture and of a pinkish color.

Gambang: an archaic iron-keyed instrument played only at cremations.

Gamelan: a Balinese orchestra.

Gangsa: a metal-keyed instrument which is usually hit with a mallet held in the right hand, the keys being damped with the fingers of the left hand. Certain types of gangsas are played with mallets in either hand.

Garoeda: a mythical bird.

Goenoeng: mountain.

Goenoeng Agoeng: literally, "great mountain." The Goenoeng Agoeng is the highest mountain in Bali and is sacred to the Balinese.

Goesti: the title of a member of the third caste.

Kain: a strip of cloth, often batik, wound about the waist and extending below the knees. It is the principal article of clothing for both men and women.

xiii

Kepeng: an ancient Chinese coin worth approximately one-fifteenth of a cent in American money. It is the common money of the Balinese.

Kliang: the elected chief of a village or a society.

Koelkoel: a hollowed or slotted log which is beaten to call people together for meetings or in emergencies.

Lamak: a panel with designs in dark green palm leaf, woven into a lighter palm leaf background. It is used as a temple decoration or outside of house gates on great feast days.

Leyak: a person versed in black magic, who can assume various forms and is capable of doing great harm in the community.

Linga: the Phallic symbol of Shiva.

Lontar: a book in which the text and illustrations are engraved onto sections of leaf from the lontar palm.

Mantra: an esoteric and powerful spoken formula.

Meroe: a pagoda with from three to eleven roofs.

Moekoer: a ceremony performed forty-two days after cremation, which results in the final release of the spirit of the dead person from his earthly bonds.

Naga: a mythical serpent or dragon.

Padoe Raksa: an ornamental gateway leading to the inner courtyard of a temple.

Paras: a soft sandstone.

Patih: a prime minister.

Pedanda: a high priest.

Pemangkoe: a low caste priest who is much closer to the people and who performs a greater part of ordinary ceremonial than does the more distant pedanda.

Pendjor: a tall bamboo pole bent at the top, from which hangs a pendant ornament of palm leaf and bright colored flowers.

Poengawa: an official who governs a district, usually a relative of the radja.

Poepoetan: literally "the end"—the mass suicide of the Balinese noble families before the conquering Dutch army.

Poeri: the palace of a radja.

Radja: a native prince. The same as the British "Rajah."

Raksasa: a demon.

Rangda: literally, "a widow," more commonly a witch, the personification of all dark and evil forces.

Rejong: a musical instrument of twelve or thirteen knobbed gongs set in a narrow horizontal frame and played by four musicians.

Ringgit: a Dutch coin equal to two and one half guilders; or at par, one dollar. In appearance, it is almost exactly like an American silver dollar.

Sawah: a rice-field.

Sirih: a leaf chewed with betel-nut. It also signifies the combination of betel-nut, lime and sirih leaves, which are chewed together.

Soebak: an association of rice growers.

Soebang: a large ear-plug of rolled palm leaf or gold, worn by unmarried girls.

Tjandi Bentar: a split entrance gateway to a temple.

Tjempaka: a tree with very sweetly scented yellow flowers.

Tjeng-tjeng: cymbals.

Tjili: the stylized figure of a woman, used as a motif in the decoration of lamaks. A tjili may also be made of kepengs or of painted wood.

Toeak: a native palm beer, only slightly alcoholic.

Trompong: a musical instrument of ten knobbed gongs set in a narrow horizontal frame. It is played by one musician.

Preface

THE foundation for this book was really laid in 1932 when I first made my acquaintance with the Indies, for I knew then that I would return. Yet in July 1939, when I sailed from New York to be gone a year, I did not realize that I would spend most of my time in Bali; but a week after I had stepped ashore at Gilimanoek I knew it, and today I would ask nothing better than to return.

I went under the auspices of the Riverside Museum, and the government of the Netherlands Indies officially recognized me as an expedition. In spite of the fact that my arrival in Java, September third, 1939, coincided with the beginning of the war in Europe, everything possible was done to assist me both by the government and by individual officials.

I am indebted to several people in Bali: to Bob Koke, for the loan of his darkroom while I was at Koeta; to John Edelman, who generously turned his house upside down for my benefit when I moved into Denpasar; and to Walter Spies for his well-known hospitality and for much advice; but above all I am indebted to Rolf Neuhaus for his constant companionship and invaluable assistance. Without his help my task would have been far more difficult.

There are also many others whom I would like to thank: especially Mr. and Mrs. Louis Horch of the Riverside Museum, and Vernon Porter, the director of the Museum, who hung my photographs so magnificently.

If this book is in any way worthy of the efforts of so many people, I will be satisfied.

PHILIP HANSON HISS

New Canaan, Connecticut
October 10, 1941

BALI

1

The history of Bali is the history of the ruling class, the Hindu-Javanese
usurpers who have never shared the life of the people.

THIS morning the sun will rise out of the sea and light with fire the peak of Bali's sacred mountain. The early mist will move wraithlike along the lower slopes and issue as pale wisps of incense from the valleys, clinging to the tree tops and clothing the lowlands in a mantle of cool gray.

Out of the silence will rise the first shrill calls of the fighting cocks. Men will move sleepily, will stretch and walk out into the growing light. They will carry the bell-shaped baskets of the cocks to the roadside, will eat their bowl of cold rice in silence, and go to plow their fields. Small boys will lead flocks of ducks rhythmically goose-stepping to the rice-fields and leave them to search for eels in the shallow water. Women will make simple offerings for the house temples, and little girls will carry water from the streams in earthen jars up steep trails.

Today in Bali the sun will beat down on a sea of glistening rice-fields, upon forest-crowned mountain peaks, upon lakes and streams, upon groups of thatched roofs surrounded by mud walls among feathery coconut palms, upon shaded lanes. At its zenith there will be a slackening of activity upon this fertile oasis caught between two oceans. The peasant will pause by his rice-field to rest. The buffaloes will wallow in the cool mud. Only the market will reach its greatest activity.

As the shadows lengthen the peasant will shoulder his plow and lead his cows toward home. Other men will already be sitting in groups in the shade, fondling their fighting cocks, discussing village affairs, or listening to stories from the Indian epics. He will stop to listen. A girl will call to him. He will smile and continue on his way.

Tonight the peasant will play in the village orchestra or will watch a shadow play. Women will bring huge offerings to the temples and leave smaller ones at the crossroads. Coconut husks, crossed one over the other, will burn outside tall gates to drive away the demons. Tonight the air will be fragrant with frangipani and tjempaka blossoms; it will resound to the tinkling melodies of the gamelan; it will be made beautiful by the sight of men and women in lovely costumes of silk and gold with flowers behind their ears and in their hair—men and women who will laugh until dawn at the antics of clowns and wonder at the heroic stories of princes, gods, and demons. Wide-eyed babies at their mothers' breasts will breathe in their heritage of sound and smell and eye-filling spectacle. Gaunt dogs will snarl over chance morsels or greedily bolt offerings placed on the ground to propitiate the evil spirits. Children will watch in wonder while their brothers and sisters spin webs of gossamer sound and fragile movement in the night. Proud women will dance a solemn ritual to the rising sun.

It was so thirty-five years ago when the Dutch army was at the gates of Badoeng; it is so today when their white Queen is in exile and the Netherlands lies in ruins; it has been so for a thousand, perhaps two thousand, years. These cultured peasants, these incredible artisans, this magically gifted people have been little touched by the wars and religions and restrictions of their conquerors. They have absorbed what they would and sloughed off the rest. By passively resisting, they have always managed not only to survive but to remain essentially unchanged. All this time wars have surged in and around Bali. The various religions of Java have become the religions of the Balinese radjas, who have fought one with the other, have conquered and been conquered. The high priests have served an alien religion. There has been a veneer of Hinduism, of Buddhism, of Sivaism, of Tantricism; yet the old animism has remained. The communes of the peasants have outlived the feudal states of the radjas; the peasants themselves have outlived their rulers.

To the Balinese people, Bali is the center of the world. It is not that the Balinese doubts the existence of other lands. That is a fact he accepts, for surely the white men who have invaded his island must have originated somewhere, and Balinese literature and art speak constantly of other countries; yet the fact is of little importance. To him Bali is sufficient. He asks no more than to live and die there, to be cremated there and, if fortunate, to be reincarnated in Bali in a future life. This is the most convincing answer to those who ask, "How do you *know* that the Balinese are happy?"

They are a simple people who do not complicate their lives by telling each other lies, by trying to justify their mode of life, or by flaunting their courage in the face of fear.

They have enough to eat without the fearful struggle for existence of most oriental races; their religion is pre-eminently suited to their needs and provides the answers to all of their questions; their village government has developed within a static society for several hundred years until it is able to rule by democro-communistic methods for the greatest good; and for the individual there are no decisions to be made—all is determined by adat, law or custom which has been tested by time.

Approximately four thousand years ago the peoples of southeastern Asia, driven from their homes by tribes from the north, passed in a series of migrations along the chain of islands which forms the Indian Archipelago. Annam and Cochin China and Cambodia were not their original homes, and there are scientists who trace them back to Egypt across India, Arabia and Phoenicia and onward to America by the islands of the Pacific. Today they are often called Indonesians to distinguish them from the Malays and Papuans. In Bali they undoubtedly supplanted a still earlier race, a very primitive vedoic type such as the bushmen of Australia. The Indonesians were sun-worshippers and animists and they brought with them the culture of rice, certain domestic animals such as dogs, pigs, water-buffaloes, and chickens, and a rudimentary knowledge of iron work and pottery.

This Indonesian civilization possessed a high degree of culture but it is seldom given proper credit for its marked contributions to Balinese art and religion. It is too easily overshadowed by subsequent Hindu-Javanese cultures transferred from Java. There are also indications of direct Hindu influences on Bali, but the greatest debt is owed to the Hindu-Javanese.

When the Indonesians came to Bali, which is separated from Java by straits less than a mile and a half wide at their narrowest part, they found an island only ninety miles long and fifty miles from north to south with a high central plateau crowned by at least one active volcano. Bali is on one of the most active volcanic belts in the world and even today the threat of eruption is never absent. Rich alluvial plains slope to the Java Sea in the north and to the Indian Ocean in the south. Among the high mountains in the center of the island are several large lakes, and there are many streams. This land is ideal for the planting of rice, and rice culture has reached a perfection unexcelled anywhere else in the world. Only the western end of the island has remained uncultivated because of the lack of water. There the few remaining tigers roam. There, wild pigs and deer and multi-colored birds flourish, but there are few people or villages. West Bali has long been the buffer between the Balinese and the encroachment of the Javanese. Today the western end of the island supports a few settlements more Javanese than Balinese, and an indifferent road connects the harbor of Gilimanoek with North and South Bali, but it is not until Antosari is reached that Bali emerges in its true character.

Along the coast the waves break on beaches of volcanic sand and against coral reefs. There are no natural harbors, a fact which has played a major role in the history of the island. The people of Bali are not a nation of sailors. If the Indonesians were the parent stock from which the Polynesians, those astonishing navigators, sprang, it is even more strange that the Balinese should have turned from the water, yet it is a fact that dislike of the sea is ingrained in them. To them everything that is high is holy, while everything that is low is unholy, and the sea is lowest of all. It is inhabited by sharks, poisonous fishes lurking in the coral reefs, and by a thousand imagined and oft-repeated fears. All the actions of the Balinese are governed by their relation to the mountains, more especially by the Goenoeng Agoeng, their most sacred mountain, which is their point of orientation. As in many other islands, directions are not determined by north and south, but by the mountains and the sea. There are a few fishing villages, for even in Bali every rule must have its exception, but the inhabitants do not venture far from shore. On certain nights at Koeta a long line of dancing flames can be seen braving the darkness. The fishermen are lighting their fear of the unknown with torches.

Balinese history until the fifteenth century is like an intricate painting, the colors of which have faded. Of their past the peasants are entirely ignorant. They have inherited a religion, a ruling class, a literature, and a theater from India by way of Java. Of this most of the people are only vaguely aware. The key to the intricacies of literature and religion are reserved for the few. The peasant has absorbed only enough of classical Hindu drama to recognize the stock characters which inhabit all plays. Of religion, it is enough to know the simple offerings and formulas for everyday life. Ritual is a matter for the priests. The peasants' wisdom is contained in adat, the traditional secular and religious law. His thought is for the present rather than for the past or the future. The Balinese early developed a simple agricultural communalism as an answer to the complex problems posed by irrigation of the sawahs and the necessity for frequent feasts and offerings to propitiate their animistic gods. Their concept of life strives toward maximum happiness in this world.

Though the Balinese are ignorant of their history, there are indications in the records of other countries as early as the first century that Bali was not unknown to the outside world. By the tenth century it had already absorbed one great Hindu migration and a Balinese king, Erlangga, son of a Javanese radja and a princess of Bali, ruled over eastern Java. Centuries of strife followed in which Bali was alternately free and the vassal of Java, but toward the end of the fifteenth century the great Hindu-Javanese dynasty of Madja-pait succumbed to ever-increasing pressure from the Mohammedan states. Unable to defend itself in Java, its entire culture was transplanted to Bali, and a Javanese king became master of the island. The Mohammedans never penetrated the Balinese fastness, and for four hundred years the culture of Madjapait developed undisturbed. Peace, which is necessary to the growth of art, fused the elements of the Indonesian and Hindu-Javanese cultures into a civilization at once simple in its basic concepts and tremendously complex in its art and religious ritual. These centuries of isolation made it possible to establish a stable society in which the problems of the individual and the community were equilibrated. Bali presents the unusual example of a nation in which private property is recognized—but not to the detriment of the community as a whole, where a nearly communistic economy exists beside a privileged feudal aristocracy, and where undeniable democratic procedure is followed in the election of village chiefs and in the conduct of village affairs.

Strict laws of caste governed the usurping Javanese, preventing inter-marriage with the peasantry who were of no caste, and this barrier continues to exist. It is one reason why the radjas have never been considered as truly Balinese, a part of the people. The princes continually attempted to destroy the village communities which were the basis of Balinese society, but the Balinese resisted fiercely and in most cases successfully. The radjas, forming only a small minority, were unable to enforce their will against the combined strength of the people and were not allowed to trespass too far on the village government. They remained in the capacity of tax collectors and landowners, but were never able to reduce the peasants to coolies. The Balinese have always been small farmers working their own land or the land of others for a share of the crop; they have never been wage earners.

The radjas and their courts contributed to the spectacle of Balinese life. They patronized the arts and subsidized orchestras, dance societies, painters, carvers, and weavers. One court vied with the others for the finest gamelan or the most skilled legong. Splendid palaces were built, and the radjas dressed in colorful cloths and wore magnificent jewelled krisses. They represented themselves to the people as of divine origin, identified with the heroes of Indian legend, who by this time the Balinese had come to accept as the forefathers

of their own deified ancestors, and the peasants were content so long as the integrity of
their communes remained undisturbed.

The princes waged wars one against the other and against the neighboring island of
Lombok, which they conquered in 1740, but the peasants continued to plow their fields,
and the fighting fell to the warrior caste. The Brahmans attempted to proselytize the peasants and educate them to Hindu ways through the Wajang Koelit, the shadow play so often
prescribed by ritual, but the ancient animism of the Indonesians was stronger than the
formal Hindu religion. These people had a strange way of distilling the essence from what
was offered them and leaving the dross. They had remained essentially untouched when
the Dutch first entered their world.

Cornelius Houtman, in command of a Dutch fleet, discovered Bali in 1597 and was
well received by the radja, but the Dutch were just then entering into a contest with the
Portuguese and the English for control of East Indian trade. Though Bali was reported as a
paradise, the practical Dutch were more interested in the transmutation of spices into gold,
and Bali, possessing little of value to these adventurers, was allowed to retain its integrity
for another three hundred years. The Dutch East India Company, a coalition of the strong-
est existing companies then trading in the Indies, was formed in 1602 for the exploitation of
all lands between India and China. For nearly two centuries its policies of brutality and
money-lust were to be the grave of thousands of natives. Rapine and slaughter were to
spread over three million square miles of land and sea. In Bali, agents of the company
vainly sought to gain favor with the radjas. Failing that, they attempted to bribe the Radja
of Lombok with promises of help if he should renounce allegiance to Bali, but without suc-
cess. After almost two centuries of misrule, the charter of the Honourable East India Company was renounced, and the Indian Empire collapsed. France had invaded Holland; war
with England was imminent; and the "civilization" of the East India Company had made
so little impression on the inhabitants of the islands of the East Indies that by the end of the
eighteenth century Portuguese was still more frequently spoken in Batavia than Dutch. By
1796 the Indies, except for Java and Ternate, had fallen to the English, and in 1811 Sir
Stamford Raffles conquered the former almost without a struggle. An era of enlightened
rule seemed about to begin, but in 1814 Java was returned to Holland. Raffles' famous
book, *The History of Java*, however, remains a monument to the time. In it he speaks of
Bali as the preserver of Hindu-Javanese culture.

It was natural that the Dutch should make every effort to consolidate their empire, should seize any pretext that would yield them a foothold from which to launch their armies, for in those days open aggression was frowned upon, and to justify their actions even to themselves they had to embrace a cause. Motives to satisfy both conscience and desire, however, were not hard to find.

The nineteenth century saw the invasion of North Bali on a flimsy pretext obviously magnified for the occasion. This invasion was successful and was followed by the conquest of Lombok. The radjas and their retainers were brave men, but they were no match for repeating rifles and modern cannon. The old Radja of Lombok was exiled to Java where he soon died of sorrow, yet there were those who could not even then foresee the inevitable end. In 1900 the Radja of Gianjar appealed to the Dutch for help against the states of Badoeng, Bangli and Kloengkoeng, which were allied against him. The Dutch promptly annexed his territory. The denouement was six years in coming and was precipitated by the looting of a small Chinese steamer driven ashore on the coast of Sanoer. Representations were made by the Dutch government which were refused, and an army was landed not far from the scene of the wreck. The following morning this force was attacked by Balinese with spears, which were naturally unavailing against Dutch rifles. The Balinese peasant, though troubled by this disturbance of his peace, did not consider the misfortunes of the Radja his own, and remained aloof. The ordinary Dutch soldier was bewildered and not a little dismayed by the ferocity of the primitively armed Balinese. He fired hesitantly to save his own life. He was the uncomprehending tool of Imperialism. The real struggle was between the Radja and the Dutch government.

On the morning of September 20, 1906, the Dutch army moved on Badoeng under cover of bombardment by the fleet, but the Radja had long since recognized his cause as hopeless and had gathered about him two thousand of his followers for a fight to the end. He would not die in exile like the Radja of Kombok; he would instead teach these marauding white men a lesson in courage and in the meaning of freedom that they would not soon forget.

To one who understands the Balinese temperament, what happened that morning only thirty-five years ago will seem neither strange nor terrible, but to the Dutch soldiers it was a scene of abiding horror. The men, women, and children of the Radja's court shared a curious exaltation at the thought of death. Once they had dedicated themselves they acted as though they were already dead, as though the sacrifice of their bodies was but the shadow of reality. With increasing intensity they possessed the characters which they would play. Many dances in Bali are but the offering of the body of the dancer to the gods; their drama is a struggle of good and evil: their life and now their death would be a dedication. They had no fear or regrets; only an increasing certainty that death was preferable to life without liberty and a conviction that self-immolation was but the prelude to rebirth.

As in a trance they dressed in white as priests for a temple feast. Dreamlike, then in a frenzy, the gamelans played. For hours the courts were alive with people coming and going. Gold and jewels flashed in the early sunlight, krisses and golden spears were everywhere. Yet beneath this tumult there was peace in the eyes of the people. In their hearts was an abiding faith which directed the bodies of these men and women from whom the renounced soul had already fled.

In the morning the Dutch army was halted by the astonishing spectacle of a column come out to meet them, an army of men and women dressed in costumes resplendent with gold and precious stones, advancing quietly, as though the white men did not exist. Suddenly the tension burst and the leaders hurled themselves at the soldiers. Volley after volley rang out; men and women fell, the Radja among them; but these impassioned people cared nothing for the white men. Death was theirs to embrace, and when the bullet failed the kris did not. Mothers killed their children, husbands their wives, and a great pile of corpses grew where the Radja had fallen. More were slain by their own hand and the krisses of their friends than by the guns of the Dutch. Crimson stains spread over the white garments and spilled into the dust. This was the end—poepoetan.

There were to be other poepoetans. Two years later Kloengkoeng presented a similar spectacle. The Dutch were now masters of all Bali.

But to the peasant it made no difference.

2

A compromise between communalism [1] and communism,[2] democracy,[3] and feudalism.[4]

THE history of four thousand years has been reduced in the first chapter to less than four thousand words, for history is but the background against which we view the present, and the culture of Bali more than any other is alive today.

This culture was imported by the Indonesians and was greatly enhanced by the contributions of India and Java. It is common to hear that Bali today is what Madjapait, the last great Hindu-Javanese civilization, was five hundred years ago, which is to say that the Balinese have added nothing. This is not so. The Balinese are a highly gifted people, who have absorbed a great many foreign ideas and adapted them to their needs, but in so doing they have added something entirely their own. The culture of two peoples drawing inspiration from the same source suggests certain parallels, but Balinese dancing, music, architecture, and religion are far more vital than those of the Javanese even in their prime. The history of Balinese culture is often obscure because of the many forces acting upon it. There were, however, special conditions which contributed to that culture and which made

[1] "A theory of government which advocates the widest extension of local autonomy for each locally definable community." OED
[2] "A theory which advocates a state of society in which there should be no private ownership, all property being vested in the community and labour organized for the common benefit of all members; the professed principle being that each should work according to his capacity and receive according to his wants." OED
[3] "That form of government in which the sovereign power resides in the people as a whole, and is exercised either directly by them or by officers elected by them." OED
[4] "A system of polity based on homage and service to a superior lord, by whom land is granted and in whom the ownership remains." OED (combined definition)

the attainment of it logical. But how can it exist in a world given over to chaos and destruction?

The purely physical reasons for Balinese survival are easily stated. Bali is an insignificant island in an outlying section of the world. It has no natural resources in sufficient quantities to tempt attack on the vast Dutch colonial empire nor has it any strategic importance, being without either good harbors or good airports. Should it fall to foreign aggression, it would be as additional spoils in the rich booty of Java, Borneo or Sumatra.

Since the poepoetans the Dutch have shown surprising good sense in their administration of the island. They have taken charge of all business and diplomatic relations with the outside world, thus relieving the Balinese of a burden to which they had been subjected since their position of isolation was destroyed, and to which they are not equal; but the Dutch have done little to disturb the communal system, which is the backbone of Balinese society. They have substituted Dutch courts for the courts of the radjas, but the administration of simple justice remains with the desa, and the peasant has shown as much ingenuity in avoiding foreign justice as he did in the past. At first the Dutch reduced the radjas to the status of regents and then gave back their original titles to them, but as Radja or Regent they are controlled by the Dutch government and "advised" by the Resident. Dutch rule, though rudely initiated, has been an advantage to the peasant who is freer from oppressive taxation and princely whims than he was in the past. Thus he has not only been able to survive, but has actually improved his position.

Rice was introduced into Bali at a very early time and became, as in so many Oriental countries, the staple of diet. Food is undoubtedly man's first need, all other considerations becoming insignificant beside it. But rice has also pointed a way of life to the Balinese; its culture has demanded skill in engineering, foresight, patience, and community effort. It is the most prominent feature of every Balinese landscape and its colorful growth forms the physical background against which Balinese life is projected.

Imagine a translucent yellow tinged with green, not chartreuse, not citron, but borrowing from both: that is the young rice close-packed in the nurseries. Space each shoot a handbreadth and the yellow-green is still there but is tempered with russet, sienna and sepia from the earth, and blue reflected from the sky: that is the same shoots transplanted in the sawahs. Imagine a transition from apple green to light chrome green to ecru: that is the rice from planting to maturity. Then imagine these colors set side by side, young rice next to the soft earth, rice ready to be harvested against a nursery, flooded sawahs against waving shoots knee-high: add to this the more sober green of the trees, the chocolate ooze of the newly-planted fields, the white roads and small splashes of crimson and ochre, saffron and rose and violet beneath a sky shading from palest blue to sapphire. These are the rice-fields of Bali, a panorama of the seasons in a single kaleidoscopic landscape.

Elaborate ceremonies of purification accompany each phase of work in the fields, offerings are made to the gods and the demons, and the harvest is celebrated by feasts and music. Certain days are set apart for the planting of rice; a prescribed time must elapse between the time when the water is let into the sawahs and when the plowing begins, between plowing and planting, and between planting and when the water is drained off; women may not plant rice, but they always help at the harvest: there are a thousand rules and superstitions which make rice culture at once a science and a colorful spectacle.

As the time for the harvest approaches, great care must be taken so that birds or mice do not spoil the grain, and elaborate networks of scarecrows, clappers and, pinwheels are set out. In the country near Tabanan, huge drums are pulled through the fields by crowds of men who also beat hollow bamboos with short sticks to scare away the demons. In the fields there are always rice temples and little shrines with fresh offerings fashioned from palm leaves and flowers. Rice is one of the most compelling forces in the life of the people.

The irrigation of a country where rice is grown in apparently every available space, from the summits of hills to the sea, is a difficult feat. Sawahs cling to the precipitous sides of canyons, rock must be excavated, aqueducts built, and water led through a maze of miniature cascades from the highest to the lowest level. All this has been accomplished without European advice or tools, in a manner that European methods could not improve, but to do so took a vast amount of organization. The problem of co-operation, not only within the village but between as many villages as received their water from a single source, must have occurred while Balinese society was still in a primitive and flexible state, and it was solved by the formation of soebaks, associations of rice growers in which all decisions were reached by democratic method, the vote of the majority. The notion of absolute ownership of property had to be abandoned, but this was not difficult, for to the Balinese the true ownership of all property rests in the gods, who allow mortals to work the land only so long as they are pleased with their conduct and their offerings. Individual ownership of property is recognized only so long as the land is used to the advantage of the community: a person may not refuse to cultivate his fields, and if he owns more land than he can work alone he must share the crop with whoever helps him, rather than pay a wage. Even his house is built on land which eventually is owned by the community. This attitude toward private ownership is an extension of our own right to condemn property if public interest out-weighs that of the individual.

The soebak, likewise, was an extension of the democratic method, for membership in it was compulsory, and though a headman was elected by the majority, he was compelled to serve even though he might prefer not to. In this way the soebak was assured the services of its most valuable members. Community interests were paramount in all cases, and this principle was applied to the village group. Religious observance speedily developed along the same lines as the soebak and desa, for communal effort was necessary to build the tem-ples and to maintain them, to prepare the feasts, and to fulfill the elaborate ritual of cre-mation. The Balinese found the concept of democratic communalism with a near-commu-nistic attitude toward property so satisfactory that they developed a passion for societies, which now cover all fields of endeavor.

The accident of geography made an agricultural life possible for the Balinese. The fer-tile fields yield two large crops of rice a year and the climate remains at a constant tempera-ture so that planting can be done at any time and the fields rotated in such a way that the water supply is always sufficient. There being no well-marked seasons, work is constant, and a moderate amount of it assures a good living, yet the fact that agricultural implements are primitive and work communally arranged makes it impossible for the individual to be-come lazy. Bali is not a garden of Eden where man does not have to work. Balinese civiliza-tion is, instead, the product of centuries of planned living. Bamboo is another product of geography which influences Balinese life greatly. Without it the Balinese would have dif-ficulty in manufacturing many articles very simply made by its use; might in fact never have made them at all, and their art and music would be the loser. It is used for dozens of indispensable articles of everyday life and is supposed to possess great magic powers.

An agricultural people have the advantage of leading a healthy outdoor life and the Balinese have been fortunate in the fertility of their island. They have become a magnifi-cently proportioned race, hardy and muscular, with broad shoulders and narrow hips. From early childhood the women have carried heavy weights on their heads and the men have carried even heavier ones on their shoulders, and this has given them effortless control of their muscles; their movement is a transition from one sculpturesque pose to another. But agriculture has meant more to the Balinese than healthy bodies; it has meant healthy nerves, a moderate tempo at which to live, time for reflection, time for niceties which lift life above mere existence; and above all, it has made them self-sufficient; it has freed them from dependence on the outside world, and it has made communalism possible.

Communalism is one of those ideal states which too often work better in theory than in practice for the reason that man is an imperfect being who rarely looks on his neighbors' fields without coveting them, but the Balinese peasant is by nature peace-loving and for this reason was able to build innumerable small communities, each complete within itself, which settled disagreements in a peaceful and civilized manner. Communalism makes possible strict attention to local needs; conditions are recognized and taken care of by the people who are most closely affected by them; officials are immediately responsible to the people, and in Bali every man casts his vote in a community small enough so that the issues are plain and are such that he can understand them.

The desa, the communal village-state, functions in much the same way as the soebak. Every married man, and in Bali this means almost every man of marriageable age, must join the desa council. He cannot refuse, for refusal would mean the seizure of his land and his expulsion from the village. Public opinion is a powerful thing, and in Bali it is wielded in the interests of the common good. To be expelled from the community is equal to life imprisonment if not death. A man "declared dead" is an outcast to whom no one in the village may so much as speak. He is denied all the benefits of village life, even the necessities of life itself, and no other village will admit him. As most land in Bali is cultivated, he is faced with life in a few malarial spots in the company of other outcasts, or death, and death is often preferable, so accustomed is he to work and play in the company of others. It is no wonder that most persons prefer co-operation, which in most cases is a pleasant thing, to such a fate.

All matters of village policy are decided by the desa council, and at meetings every member must be present. These meetings are presided over by a kliang, or chief, who has been elected by a majority vote. Like the chief of the soebak, his position is one of honor. He cannot refuse to serve, but he may be removed if he is unsatisfactory. The position of kliang is hereditary only if a son is the equal of his father. To be a Balinese citizen one must be a responsible member of the community, willing at all times to serve in any capacity without pay.

Life within the desa moves effortlessly and seemingly without direction. The Balinese have a real feeling of equality, a truly democratic outlook. They never presume to order one another about. No one seems to take any responsibility for anything, yet somehow things are done, perhaps not at the scheduled time, but certainly with the least fuss. Time, in the sense that we attribute to it, is non-existent to the Balinese: the right time for anything is when everyone is ready. What matter if it is noon or midnight? Time is not so precious that men must be its slaves. It is pleasant to sit in the shade and wait, it is pleasant to laugh and talk with one's friends, to stroke one's fighting cocks, to chew sirih, or to sleep. The ability of primitive races, or those living in simple surroundings, to relax, to sleep, and to wake when rested, and to live free from a daily schedule is one of their most precious gifts. It is the heritage of all animals, and only civilized man has seen fit to make an automaton of himself.

Economic security in the Balinese community is assured, for each person has his place in the social order. Should misfortune or sickness prevent him from working, he knows that he will be cared for until he is able to work again. In Bali no one goes hungry. Balinese life is, therefore, one of economic security based on an abundance of natural resources distributed among an active agricultural people. It is one of economic equality because of the comparative insignificance of material possessions. A simple kain, or cloth wrapped about the waist and extending below the knees, is the usual dress for either men or women, and it is a sufficient wardrobe for all ordinary occasions. There is nothing in a house or its furnishings which is not made of clay, bamboo, palm, or wood; all readily available materials quickly put together with assistance from other villagers, who expect no reward other than assistance when they need it. A sawah may be inherited but a man without one may receive one from the village or he may cultivate someone else's for a share of the rice. Other fields are owned by the village association and these are worked communally and the rice distributed according to the work done. Economic inequality is nowhere great, and there are few distinguishing marks to call attention to the differences which do exist. The basis for envy and dissatisfaction is reduced to a minimum.

The princes are an exception, but they are considered by the people to be a race apart. This princely class tried to destroy the functions of the desa with the object of substituting a feudal system. Fortunately, by this time the principles of communalism were so ingrained that the princes were not able seriously to dislocate the desa government except in a few communities where the desa had become large and unwieldy. This led to the re-formation of these desas into bandjars, smaller units within the desa, which assumed most of the powers of the desa and were patterned after it. The bandjars fulfilled the original intention of the desa and restored flexibility and intelligent co-operation to those communities which had grown too large, and in turn offset the power which the princes had gained.

The laws governing the actions of the people within the desa, soebak, and temple were the product of the wisdom of many generations distilled for centuries during which the basic problems remained the same. These laws eventually became perfectly adapted to the needs of the community and were considered as adat, tradition. The wisdom of generations is always superior to that of the individual, and it is essential to the orderly process of development that reform be based on a proper knowledge of what has gone before. Balinese

Boats at Serangan

Koelkoel

Rice-fields near Gitgit

3

4   *Rice-fields at Dusk*

Harvesting Rice 5

6   *Planting Rice*

Threshing Rice   7

8   *Girls Bathing*

Old Woman Spinning 9

Man Carrying Fighting Cocks

Man with Fighting Cock 11

Fishing Boat

Bull Racing   13

14   *Climbing for Coconuts*

Carrying Coconuts

16   *Fisherman Throwing Net*

reverence for adat is founded on a sound pragmatism. The truth of an idea can only be tested by the results of its practical application, and adat has worked supremely well for those who have followed it. The Balinese are the happiest people in the world!

Adat provides the answer to all the questions posed by religion and daily life. It is not because Balinese life is without problems that the people are happy, but because there are no problems which have not already been answered and the answers incorporated into adat law. There is no possibility of choice, where every action has been pre-ordained by experience.

Adat is predicated on the common good. It is completely opposed to individualism. Why, then, is the individual so completely happy and so well adjusted? Freedom, meaning the right of the individual to do as he pleases without consideration for others, exists nowhere in the Orient. It is, instead, thought of in the Hegelian sense of spiritual self-fulfillment. Freedom without restraint would, in Bali, be regarded as license, and license is debilitating to both body and soul.

Liberty and freedom are two of the most abused words in the English language. Freedom of the individual within a very strict moral code may even be preferable to the wider concept of freedom which is ours. Absolute freedom is an ideal to be striven toward, but the Balinese understand that if an ideal cannot be reached, it either loses its potency or has the effect of making the individual unhappy. A society in which many of the problems are already answered leaves fewer uncertainties to be solved by the individual, who is less confused and consequently happier. In America the original concept of democracy assumed a certain responsibility of the individual to the community. In times of war or other great national calamities, we strive toward unity of purpose and admit the necessity for the submersion of individual freedom into the greater cause. During such times we are taken out of ourselves and glory in self-sacrifice. We reserve our deepest admiration for gallantry, which is the complete subservience of an individual to a cause. The Balinese go a step further. They apply this principle to their entire life.

3

A nation of cultured peasants.

THE typical Balinese village is an island of dark green leaves in a shimmering sea of rice-fields. It is usually by the banks of a small stream which has cut deeply into the soft sandstone, or by a wide, shallow river, boulder-strewn and flecked with the pale foam of tumbling waters. White ribbons of roads and trails lead to this village; and at all times of the day and night, but especially in the early morning and the late afternoon, the roads are alive with traffic. Occasionally an automobile or an ancient bus hurtles by, raising great clouds of dust, but for the most part the goods of Bali still are transported on the shoulders of men and on the heads of women. A trail in the grass beside the road, worn smooth by the passing of thousands of feet, is unmistakable proof of this. Every third day, a market is held in each village and men and women from the surrounding countryside come to sell or trade their wares: sugar cane, cakes, vegetables, or livestock, ducks, or young pigs bound tightly in cylindrical palm-leaf baskets. There are others with bulky material and tremendous piles of pottery set at crazy angles—seemingly impossible burdens—yet the people travel at an easy, ambling gait which is not a walk, but neither is it a run. In this way they cover surprising distances; twenty-five to thirty miles a day, with heavy loads, is not unusual. The roads wind along the edges of sawahs and zigzag up the mountains, where on one side may be a perpendicular retaining wall and on the other, abruptly terraced fields; the natural contours divided into a hodgepodge of unequal plots, some so tiny that they scarcely seem worth cultivating. In the corner of a rice-field there may be an offering of flowers, and little figures of plaited bamboo and palm-leaf. Steel bridges now span the deepest ravines, where the people once had to wind down tortuous paths to the river and up again on the far side. But these bridges are so narrow that an

19

automobile cannot pass a person on foot, and the rickety charabancs, driven at reckless speed and bulging with people, freight, and livestock, seem to squeeze through only by a miracle. At the sound of a motor, people on the bridge scatter, hastening off the far end, or wedging themselves between the girders.

Inside the village, the streets are dark tunnels beneath the over-arching trees. The glaring white of the sun-baked roads here becomes a pleasant twilight. On either side of the street are deep drainage ditches and beyond them, in an unbroken line, rise high mud walls crowned with thatch and punctuated by tall gateways. These gateways are reached from the street by palm logs placed across the ditches. Lean dogs leap in and out of the gateways and children play by the roadside. Fighting cocks in their baskets make a pattern of sound and color close to the walls, where they have been placed so that they can watch the passersby. Sway-backed pigs with triangles of wood about their throats look out over the high sills, or roam in the streets. Red hibiscus and purple bougainvillea rise above the walls and perhaps there will be a dead cock on a gateway, his wings pegged out, his long tail drooping in an iridescent pattern of reddish, green, and black tones. This is an offering against sickness in the house.

Many of the smaller villages do not have a market enclosure. Instead, the women set up their small tables beneath giant banyan trees, which, in most villages, are on one side of the village square. The market is a social as well as a business affair. The women have the opportunity of talking to one another, of discussing household affairs, and of bargaining. Business is transacted almost entirely with kepengs, small Chinese copper coins with holes in the center, which are worth about a fifteenth of a cent in American money. They are carried in long strings, and it is a credit to the mathematical abilities of the people that they can do business with them at all. Those Balinese who come into contact with Europeans are acquainted with Dutch money, but in many districts it is not acceptable. Nowhere in the market are voices raised above the level of conversation, except in laughter. Only the snarling of the dogs over every stray morsel disturbs the peace; these hideous skeletons covered with huge, ulcerous sores are everywhere, and together with the pigs, they are the scavengers of Bali. These dogs are so much a part of Balinese life that it is doubtful whether their existence is even noticed as they wander about among the offerings at a temple feast, fight viciously together during a ceremony, or walk under a dancer's feet during a performance. They are never fed, but exist on stray morsels, offerings that are placed on the ground for evil spirits, and by hunting. But they play their part in the economy of the island. The year that an effort was made by the Dutch officials to reduce their numbers, there was a plague of rats in the rice-fields. The dogs are useful to the Balinese, who would, in any case, hesitate to offend them, as they might be the incarnation of evil spirits. This conception may have arisen from the fact that the dogs immediately consume all offerings placed on the ground.

At any gathering, be it a dance, a cockfight or at the market-place, one notices great variety in the faces of the people. Probably the most common type of face is rather full, the eyes set wide apart and obliquely in the face and tapering to the outside, though at a lesser degree than those of the Chinese. The eyelids are full, the lashes long, and the eyebrows are at a more acute angle than the eyes. The nose is slightly flattened at the bridge, and the nostrils are dilated. The mouth is sensuous but not over-large. The hair may or may not grow low on the forehead. The ears of all women, and of some men, are pierced; the holes in the women's ears being gradually expanded by increasing the size of long, coiled strips of bamboo, until huge soebangs, earplugs, an inch in diameter and three inches long, made of gold or silver and set with semi-precious stones, can be worn. In their youth the hair of all Balinese is black, and their eyes are dark. Individuals vary considerably from this basic type. Many men and women, especially those of the higher castes, have more refined features; the nose straight, the mouth small, the cheek-bones high, the whole face longer and narrower than the ordinary. Some of the people have distinctly Mongolian features, and there are a very few who have the curly hair and the thick lips of the Papuan. Older men and women often have features closely resembling common European types. There are virtually no half-castes in Bali, for, due to their religion, Balinese women seldom marry foreigners, and the men never do. There are only two or three children on the entire island who are half white, and perhaps a few dozen who are half Chinese. Both men and women have broad shoulders that taper to the waist, which is very small, and most of them have practically no hips. The women are beautifully sculptured, having sufficient flesh to cover their bones adequately, yet few are fat. Their breasts are usually full and firm, and their carriage erect, due in part to having carried loads on their heads from their earliest childhood. What is more, they do not lose their figures as they grow older. It is common to see a woman who, from behind, has the figure of a young girl, and discover from her face that she must be fully forty or fifty years old. The men have the beautiful, long, flowing muscles of dancers, and they too are seldom fat.

Like most other races in this part of the world, the older Balinese men and women chew sirih, a combination of sirih leaves, lime and betel-nut. This turns their teeth black and the inside of their mouths red. The scene of any Balinese meeting might easily be a battleground, so nearly does the sirih match the color of blood as it lies in little pools in the white dust. Many of the younger men and girls have given up this habit and have beautiful, white, even teeth, and some of the others who still chew sirih polish their front teeth with brick dust, which makes them white.

There is a great variety of costumes among the Balinese. It is, in fact, astonishing that so much individuality can be expressed within the limitations of everyday dress. Both the men and women wear batik kains imported from Java, and in addition to this, the women wear underskirts, and sashes tied about their waists. Twined in their hair, women wear long scarfs or, as is the modern fashion, cheap bath towels, which are also used to cover the breasts on occasion. The men wear squares of batik, bound around their heads and brought to a peak in the front, but every man has an individual way of wearing his headdress, or of wrapping his kain. The men often complete their costumes with scarlet hibiscus flowers behind their ears, the women with frangipani and tjempaka blossoms in their hair. Contrary to this very simple dress, the ceremonial costumes of the people are tremendously elaborate. For temple feasts and other special occasions, the Balinese women wear costumes of bro-caded and gold appliquéd silk. The underskirt is worn long in front and carried between the legs, forming a short train. The breasts are bound about with yards of cloth which is, in turn, covered with gold or brocade work. Their hair is a mass of flowers done in a variety of ways, gold flowers frequently being combined with fresh ones. The women use a white rice powder on their faces, and a heavy black makeup on their eyebrows. The men wear a white kain gathered in front and hanging to the ground. Over this is a brocaded cloth which falls open, disclosing the draped end of the kain. This cloth is held in place with a scarf, bound under the armpits, which also holds the ceremonial kris, worn in the back with its hilt projecting just above the left shoulder. The young girls are miniature copies of their mothers, but the small boys, except when they are mere babies, are seldom elaborately dressed. In fact, until they are six or seven years old, they rarely wear anything at all.

A Balinese home is a compound entirely surrounded by a high mud wall topped with thatch. One enters through a tall doorway which fronts on the street, and on either side of which are small shrines built into the masonry. Directly behind the gateway there is usu-ally a protective wall which screens the courtyard from the street and presumably keeps the evil spirits from entering. Within this courtyard are scattered various buildings; the most important being those of the house temple, which are set apart in a small section enclosed by a wall. These shrines are always on the side of the compound which is nearest to the mountains, and on the right side. Thus, in South Bali, the shrines are in the northeast corner of the compound; in North Bali they are in the southwest corner. Every house has its temple, dedicated to the ancestral gods, and to the sacred mountains, the Goenoeng Agoeng, and the Batoer. In the house of a poor man, shrines are small, and are usually built of bamboo with thatched roofs, but the house temple of a man of wealth may be as elaborate as many of the village temples. In addition to the house temple, there are also one or two small shrines within the courtyard, around which are clustered the buildings for eating, sleeping and entertaining. In the middle of the north side of the compound, or the side facing toward the mountain, is the only building which is entirely enclosed. It may be built of mud or brick, or, in certain sections of the island, of stone, but in all cases, its only aperture is the door leading to the central courtyard. It has no windows, nor any other means of ventilation. The inside of this building is entirely taken up by two large beds with frames of bamboo and strips of bamboo woven between the sides. Bedding may be either piles of matting or a cheap mattress. These beds are placed one on either side of the door. At night the door is kept tightly closed. The building may or may not have a verandah on the front, depending upon the wealth of the family. This house is the sleeping quarters of the head of the household and his wife. The small treasures belonging to the family are kept here, and very often money is hidden away in a hole dug in the earth floor or in a bamboo rafter slotted to admit a silver ringgit, a Dutch coin equal in value to our silver dollar at the normal rate of exchange, and resembling it very closely. Ringgits are pushed through the slot into the hollow bamboo and gravitate to the far end. There is no possible way of getting them out, except by breaking open the bamboo, which would be immediately obvious to the owner. The story is told that one very wealthy man, who owned a great many coconut trees, and sold copra to the local Chinese dealers, concealed so many ringgits in this fashion that the roof of his house collapsed. There are several other buildings within the compound, a kitchen, a rice granary, and several balés, buildings with raised platforms under roofs of thick palm thatch. These balés may be entirely open, or, as is more often the case, have walls on one or two of the sides. The largest balé is usually the living quarters and guest hall; the two smaller ones are the sleeping quarters of the relatives and children. So accustomed are the Balinese to sleeping within the protective wall of the house compound that if they must spend the night in the fields, or in a strange place, they huddle together in fear of evil spirits and leyaks, persons versed in black magic, who can assume fearful forms and can do great damage to an individual or to a community. There are also enclosures for the pigs, and here refuse is disposed of. The central courtyard is of clean swept earth. Within the compound, and outside of the central courtyard, there is a fringe of tall coconut palms and, occasionally, bread-fruit and papaya trees. Everywhere there is hibiscus and frangipani, tjempaka and bougainvillea. The Balinese have very little feeling of ownership for these flowers, and do not object if a stranger scales the house wall and picks them. Coconut trees, however, are a different matter. Fruit which falls into the street is the property of the first passerby, but many of the coconut trees throughout the island, especially in the spots more remote from the homes of their owners, are studded with sharp spikes pointed downward, which in turn are covered with matted palm leaves, so that it is impossible to climb the trees. In the daytime, the coconuts can be gathered by means of a knife attached to a long stick.

Thievery is uncommon in Bali, and doors are never locked. Any crime of the sort is quickly dealt with by the community. Europeans, however, do not come within the Balinese code, and the Balinese do not have the same attitude toward stealing from them. But such stealing is rare in any case and is usually of a very minor character. Crime is so infrequent in Bali that the jails are small and serious offenders have to be sent to the penitentiary in Java. I heard of one amusing instance of the rather informal way in which justice is meted out by the Dutch. A Balinese was convicted of some small crime, and was sentenced to serve several months in prison. The judge was in a quandary—the limited capacity of the jail was already taxed. He finally resolved the entire difficulty: "When we have room for you, I'll drop you a card and you can serve your sentence at that time," he said. And that was what happened.

The Balinese people lead a very irregular life, eating when they are hungry, or when it is convenient, and sleeping when they are tired. Food is cooked once a day by the women, and there is always cold rice in the house. Though nominally Hindus, they eat all kinds of meat, especially chicken and duck, pork and beef. Only the high priests and a few people of very high caste are forbidden to eat beef. After eating, they drink from an earthen jug with a long spout, pouring the water in a continuous stream into their mouths. This is sanitary, but it is an almost impossible feat for an European. All food is eaten from leaf plates which are later thrown away. There are therefore no dishes to be washed. The Balinese have a great variety of fruits and vegetables. Peanuts are grown in abundance and form a favorite ingredient of some of the dishes sold at the little food stands which are so common on the roads and at all feasts or dramatic performances. There are also more exotic dishes. Dragonflies are caught by children with long sticks, gummed at one end. It is a common sight to see these children in the rice-fields and on the roads, carrying strings of dragonflies which are later fried in coconut oil and eaten. In several villages to the north of Denpasar, great nets are stretched from one tall tree to another, or from a tree to the ground, in order to catch large bats. The Balinese also eat fish and small eels from the rice-fields; and for large feasts, either roast pig or huge sea turtles, cooked with spices or grated coconut, are great delicacies. Though everyday cooking is done by the women, the preparations for feasts devolve upon the men, and because of the heat, all food must be prepared the same day that it is to be eaten. Consequently, the preparations for feasts begin very early in the morning. Men may eat a bit of cold rice before going into the fields, or, if they leave very early, they take with them a portion of rice wrapped in a banana leaf. Other meals are also very irregular, but the heaviest is usually taken just after the middle of the day, or in the early afternoon. The food stands, however, are well patronized at all hours, and particularly so during feasts. It is the women's privilege to prepare food and sell it at the market-place, or wherever else there are people. Any money made in this manner belongs to her, and she may do with it as she pleases. As the women's duties about the house are not too arduous, many married women sell in this fashion, along with the younger girls.

Each morning the women and young girls prepare fresh offerings for the house shrines and other small offerings which they leave in certain spots to propitiate the evil spirits. They sweep out the house compound, bring water from the river, and cook the meal for the day. After that, they may turn to such things as weaving, the making of special offerings on feast days, food selling, and the pounding of rice. During the harvest, they also work in the fields. The women of most households spin their own thread, and weave. The weaving usually is done in one of the smaller balés, and the timber attached to one end of the warp may be fastened to the pillars of the balé, or it may be held by a special framework. The other end is fastened to a bow-shaped support which fits against the small of the woman's back. Women may weave for hours during the day if there is nothing more important to be done. At Tenganan in East Bali, there is a loose-woven cloth of which the thread of both warp and weft, before being woven, is tied and dyed to form the pattern of the finished cloth. It is known as "double ikat." This work requires an almost impossible accuracy, and it takes five years to weave a single cloth. This is so partly because this cloth is very holy and can only be woven on certain days. It is curious that the Balinese, who weave so many lovely materials and produce so many interesting cloths of their own, should do no batiking whatsoever, though all of the people on the island wear batik kains, and all of them must be imported from Java.

Lamaks, delicate strips of dark green palm leaf, woven into an abstract or conventionalized design upon a background of the yellow unopened leaf of the coconut palm, the whole forming a panel, are the necessary adjunct of every temple feast, and hang in front of all house gates, or in the house shrines, on special feast days throughout the year. During Galoengan, the great feast of the New Year, these lamaks are displayed throughout the entire island together with the graceful, drooping pendjors which line the roads, their huge palm-leaf tassels hanging from the curved ends of tall bamboo poles. Ordinary lamaks vary from a few inches to a foot in width, and from two to six feet in height, but occasionally one sees much larger ones. The making of lamaks is an art which all women must master, and it is a common sight in Bali to see women and small girls weaving the dark green leaf design into the lighter background, and pinning it in place with little pieces of bamboo. This is a decorative art, but unfortunately, both lamaks and pendjors are highly perishable, and a few days after they have been placed in the broiling tropical sun, they have wilted.

Pottery is a craft of particular interest as well as being a home industry. All pots are made of a very poor clay, which is formed and then baked in a primitive oven, the pieces being covered by rice straw, and the whole set on fire. The percentage of loss in this type of baking is very great, and the pots are fragile in any case, but as they sell for only a few cents each, they are easily replaced. The usual method for making a small bowl or jar is with the conventional potter's wheel, but this method is not practical for the manufacture of the larger bowls and huge water jugs. They are made by placing the clay on a pedestal, and walking around it while performing the same motions with the hands that are used with the revolving wheel. It is fascinating to watch a large jug being fashioned in this way, for considerable skill is required to synchronize all of the movements. There are villages which specialize in the making of pottery, and most of the large towns have a special pottery market which is held on different days from the main market.

Rice is the most important single consideration in Balinese life, and constant attention must be paid to the fields. As there are two crops of rice a year, and as one field may be ready for the harvest when the next one is being planted, plowing, planting, and harvesting are an everyday affair. After the crops have been harvested, the fields are allowed to lie fallow for a specified length of time, and the stubble and the rice straw are burned and fertilize the soil. Later the fields are dug up by men, working five or six together, with long-handled forks, the wooden teeth set at right angles to the shaft. Then the water is let in and the sawah is plowed time and again with crude wooden plows and smoothed over with wooden blades pulled behind teams of bulls or carabaos.

The racing of bulls in teams of two has resulted naturally from using them for plowing the fields. Bull racing is particularly popular in the section around Soewoeg in North Bali. The racing bulls are magnificent beasts, varying in color from a light brown to a near black. Their legs are white, as is a section of their hind quarters, and their hides are sleek and gleaming from constant care. When they race they are bedecked with great crowns of perforated buffalo hide covered with gold leaf and painted with brilliant colors. Their yokes are of carved and gilded wood, and each team has three to five banners fluttering from its yoke. Each bull wears about his neck a huge wooden bell, three and a half to four feet across, painted black and with a floral design in gold leaf, or of natural polished wood. These bells have two wooden clappers which resound dully when the bulls race. The driver perches precariously behind on the framework above the wooden blade that is used for smoothing the fields. Bull races are now frequently held on fields of hard-packed dirt, though the races were undoubtedly originally held in the deep mud of the sawahs. Two or three teams at a time advance down the course with pennants fluttering, the noses of the bulls held up, about their fore-feet small silver bells adding their note to the already colorful spectacle. The drivers urge them on by voice, and occasionally with the end of a rope. Although the bulls attain a surprising speed for such large animals, the most interesting thing is the style with which they move, their knees held high like those of a well-trained trotting horse, their heads thrust back so that the huge bells do not knock against their upraised knees. The Balinese bet on the races in the same way that they gamble at cock-fights or cricket-fights.

Work in the fields is often begun before daylight and continued after dusk, in preference to working in the extreme heat of midday. The stubble and the rice straw are always plowed back into the fields, and constant attention is paid to the careful selection of rice for the next planting. The finest ears are selected and laid in rows in previously prepared nurseries, where they soon sprout and form a spot of brilliant color on the landscape. Later these shoots are taken out and planted eight inches apart in the flooded sawahs. After a certain period of time the water is drained off and as the rice matures, it rises breast high and the stalks are weighed down with great ears of yellow grain.

The harvesting of rice is a familiar sight: tall banners of the societies floating over the fields; long lines of men and women holding in the palms of their hands the small knives with which they cut the stalks; great piles of golden grain; women crowned with huge sheaves of rice, walking erect between the sawahs and along the roads; men following, each with two or three sheaves balanced at the ends of their carrying poles. Later one sees groups of twenty or thirty women pounding the rice in stone mortars with large, wood pestles, bouncing these pestles with one hand and catching them with the other. Two or three women are grouped about each mortar and they drop their pestles in turn in a manner that creates a rhythmic background for their work.

While the men work in the fields and the women cook and go to the markets, young girls follow their mothers and learn by imitation. Boys, or old men who are unable to do heavier work, take the flocks of ducks to the rice-fields. The ducks are guided by long bamboo poles, tufted with feathers, or with small flags at their ends. These are stuck into the soft earth of the sawah, and the ducks gather around them and remain during the entire day, without requiring further attention. The ducks are trained to remain close to the flag by tying them to the pole with a long string, and by including in each group ducks which have previously been trained. In the late afternoon the men or boys bring them home again. Young boys also tend the carabaos. They take them for their daily bath in the streams, and scrub their rough hides, or loll on their backs. Carabaos, of which there are two varieties, one a slate gray and the other an albino type with a pink skin, are used for plowing the fields in the same way as the bulls.

The Balinese man must marry before he can assume his place on the village council. He has been brought up to believe that marriage is a natural and desirable state. Generally he marries while he is still young, but there is no child marriage in Bali. A marriage may be arranged between two families when the boy and girl are babies; or a couple may decide to get married and simply go away together. One frequently hears about the spectacular Balinese kidnappings, which sometimes precede a wedding ceremony, but they have been given undue prominence. Kidnapping is usually with the consent of the bride, who is captured and abducted by a party led by the groom. Custom dictates that her parents shall then lead another party in search of the couple, who, of course, are not found. Later the parents are placated by friends of the groom, who arrange the price to be paid for the girl. After the honeymoon, the couple returns to their home and the marriage ceremony is performed. Occasionally, there are forceful abductions. Two took place during my stay in Bali. A small legong in Legian, who had just come of age, was carried off, and the affair caused considerable excitement, for the girl's parents called in the police. However, when the couple were discovered, the girl decided to stay with the boy, and they were later married. A similar affair occurred not long afterward in Denpasar, and ended in much the same way. In Bali, the girl's decision is always final. Even in cases of prearranged marriage, the girl can refuse or can arrange to be abducted by another man. If both these expedients fail, she may always have recourse to divorce.

Marriage is almost universal in Bali. Even the high priests marry and have children.

Polygamy is practiced in most communities, and it is legal for any man to have more than one wife. The first wife often welcomes a second, for it relieves her of part of the work of the household, but not every man can support a second wife. In Bali the men and the women are almost equally divided, which is another reason that polygamy is somewhat restricted. There are even a few towns in North Bali where polyandry is practiced. Generally speaking, the entire attitude of the Balinese to marriage and sexual relationship is free and non-sentimental, but not promiscuous. The Balinese love children, yet the average couple have no more than three or four. For this reason the strength of the women is conserved, and the race as a whole is healthier.

In a community where the responsibility of the individual to his neighbors is every-where stressed, it is only natural that discipline should begin at an early age, with a height-ened realization within the individual of his position in the family. The Balinese child is born into a society in which his position has already been predetermined, and his responsi-bilities fixed. As soon as children are weaned, they are left in the care of older children and become a part of an independent child society. They are given their own money, and, when they are away from home, they buy their own food. They organize their own play groups, and explore the village in the company of other children. Babies are not allowed to cry, and when they become fretful they are immediately given the breast. Neither are they permitted to crawl on the ground. In fact, until they are several months old, they are not allowed to touch the ground at all. To crawl is to act as an animal, and the Balinese seek to avoid this in every way possible. Balinese children are never spanked—they are reasoned with. If this is not sufficient, the disapproval of their friends soon changes their attitude. A sense of responsibility is quickly passed on from the older children to the younger ones. In Bali, even the children seem to have learned the secret of harmonious living. During many months in Bali, I never saw a fight among either children or adults, nor even a near fight. As might be expected, there is a certain amount of domination of the younger children by the older ones, but the younger ones in turn soon have others whom they can dominate, and the youngest, if he is too hard pressed, may appeal to an adult.

In addition to this life within their own age group, Balinese children quickly learn by example the trades of their fathers, or the household duties of their mothers. They are taken everywhere by their parents and are, from a very early age, accustomed to an adult society in which they are treated as individuals with certain rights, and, in turn, certain responsi-bilities of their own. There is a minimum of book learning and theory, and a maximum of practical education. Education of this type is acceptable to children. They enjoy working in the company of their parents, and everything that they learn is justified in their eyes because it is immediately applicable to their daily life. Balinese children early reach a maturity of outlook which in no way detracts from their childlike qualities or their sense of fun. They have all the prankish characteristics of the children of other races, but, due to their added sense of responsibility, they are seldom malicious. Children, of course, share also in the artistic and religious life of the community. No dance or dramatic performance, at whatever hour of the day or night, is without its child spectators, who sit in animated groups, or, when they become drowsy, sleep between the knees of other children. Girls of eight are already accomplished dancers, and boys of the same age, who have learned the elements of music from their fathers during performances of the gamelan, are equally proficient musicians. These children are born into an artistic environment, and their heredity is one of many hundreds of years of artistic accomplishment. Little wonder that they bear within them the seeds of a full life.

The Balinese have very rudimentary ideas about medicine. They avoid a sick person whenever possible, believing that he draws from their own strength, and saps their vitality. They know of a few herbs which they brew into a medicine, or make into a yellow salve which is smeared upon the face and body. They have a skin disease which causes white blotches to appear on their otherwise brown skins, but this is due to a dietary deficiency and can be corrected in a few days by proper eating. Malaria is common, especially in some of the coastal districts, and many people have syphilis, though not nearly so many as is often reported. Since many of the women have taken to wearing blouses, tuberculosis has become more prevalent. The Balinese themselves have little idea of how to treat either of these diseases, or the ulcers which they sometimes get, particularly on their legs and arms. If their own rude treatment is ineffective, they may go to a Chinese doctor, who will treat them for a few cents; but only as a last resort, and usually after it is too late, will they go to an European physician. They believe that they should not interfere too much in their destiny: if it is ordained that a person should die, undue efforts to save his life will be displeasing to the spirits. For the same reason, they do not long mourn a person who has died, and will appear quite cheerful the day following the death of a favorite child or of a parent.

During the heat of the day, or after the day's work has been done, the men sit about in the cool shade of the huge banyan trees in the village squares, or by the tree-lined avenues. They take their fighting cocks from their baskets and smooth their heads or fluff out their tails. Occasionally one cock will be tested without spurs in a brief flurry with another, to whet the appetite of both for battle. The men and their brilliantly-colored roosters are inseparable. In the shade of a balé a man may read from a lontar book, while other men listen attentively, or criticize and discuss a passage, but they still hold their roosters in their arms and stroke them. Cock-fighting, aside from being a sport, has religious significance. Certain ceremonies require the spilling of blood, and cock-fighting is almost invariably the answer. Cock-fighting also satisfies the gambling instincts of the people, and provides a pleasant excuse for whiling away a few hours in the company of friends. It is a sociable pastime, and provides the men with an informal contact with one another similar to the women's meetings at the market-places. Cock-fighting has been largely banned by the Dutch, except for certain feasts when it fulfills a religious requirement. But the Balinese can see no reason why it is worse for one cock to kill another than it is for a man to butcher him. Cock-fighting, therefore, continues in a very open manner, and most of the Dutch officials have the good sense to turn their heads in the opposite direction as they pass. Cock-fights attract large crowds, and there is a good deal of confusion as matches are made and bets placed. The cocks wear spurs, often five inches long, and a lucky thrust may end a fight in short order. Once a fight has begun, if one cock runs away or refuses to fight, both cocks are placed in a wicker basket, where one is quickly killed. The loser is often quartered on the spot and unsentimentally given to the women to be cooked.

Many of the Balinese take a great interest in cricket-fights, which are like cock-fights in miniature. Crickets are kept in slotted tubes of bamboo with little doors at one end. Two of these bamboo cages are placed end to end and the doors withdrawn. The battle ends with the death of one of the combatants.

Cock-fighting, cricket-fighting, and bull racing are the only Balinese sports, but several games are played wherein pebbles are moved from one section to another of a design drawn on the ground. There are also a few card games, and a game where an ornamental coin is spun, and concealed by a semicircular cover placed over it. Bets are then placed as to whether it has fallen heads or tails. Whatever the sport or game in Bali, it is certain to involve gambling.

The temple is the center of village life, and their religion provides the Balinese with much of the pageantry, the feasts, the dramas, the dances, and the music which make their life so colorful. Drama, especially the shadow play, is a means of religious education, as well as a fascinating entertainment. Thus religion not only supplies the answers to men's spiritual needs, but is the basis of their social life as well.

The Balinese is a part of an unchanging world in which he fulfills a limited number of daily requirements, repeating them so often that they become a part of unconscious rather than conscious action. He is at once a farmer and an artist, an artisan and a councilman, a musician and a dancer. He is familiar with every person living in his small community and is bound to them by communal participation in all of these things, and by the common bond of religion which governs every action of his life. The village god is considered to be the ancestor of all. This worship of a common ancestor is bound up with the deification of the dead, who have become identified with the heroes of legend. The Balinese are bound by strong ties to their family in particular, to their village as a whole, and to all Balinese people. So strong is this feeling of kinship, that they constantly speak of brothers and sisters who are, in reality, no relation at all, and a childless family may borrow a child to complete their home.

Religion is so closely related to every act of his life that it is inconceivable that any Balinese could ever be persuaded to embrace another religion. To do so would destroy the very foundations of his existence, would sever his connection with his past, would undermine the basis of his pageantry, his music, his drama and his art, would leave him defenseless before a thousand nameless fears. Nevertheless, after the conquest of Bali by the Dutch, missionaries were allowed to try to convince the Balinese of the superiority of the Christian way of life. The Balinese listened, but they had no enthusiasm. Not even the terrors of hell could disturb them, for they had long since learned how to deal with demons and evil spirits. The single conversion which was made ended disastrously with the murder of the missionary, and, from that time, missionaries were banned by law from the island. But there has always been a strong church element in Holland, and pressure has been exerted upon the government to allow their return. The law has never been repealed, but recently ministers have again come to the island—ostensibly to attend to the spiritual wants of the Europeans—but various means are being used to obtain converts. Due to an increasing population, certain districts in Bali are becoming crowded. The missionaries are holding out land as a lure, people are promised free food, and the superior position of the white man is also cited to prove the greater power of Christianity. These are all time-tested ways of convincing a primitive people that the white God should be substituted

Girl of Kedaton

18   *Child*

Djanger Dancer 19

Actor

Girl

High Caste Mother and Child

Grandfather and Grandson   23

24   *Genggong Dancer*

Legong Dancer

Young Girl

Young Man   27

Girl of Asah

Girl of Bedoeloe

30   *Man with Sirih Stamper*

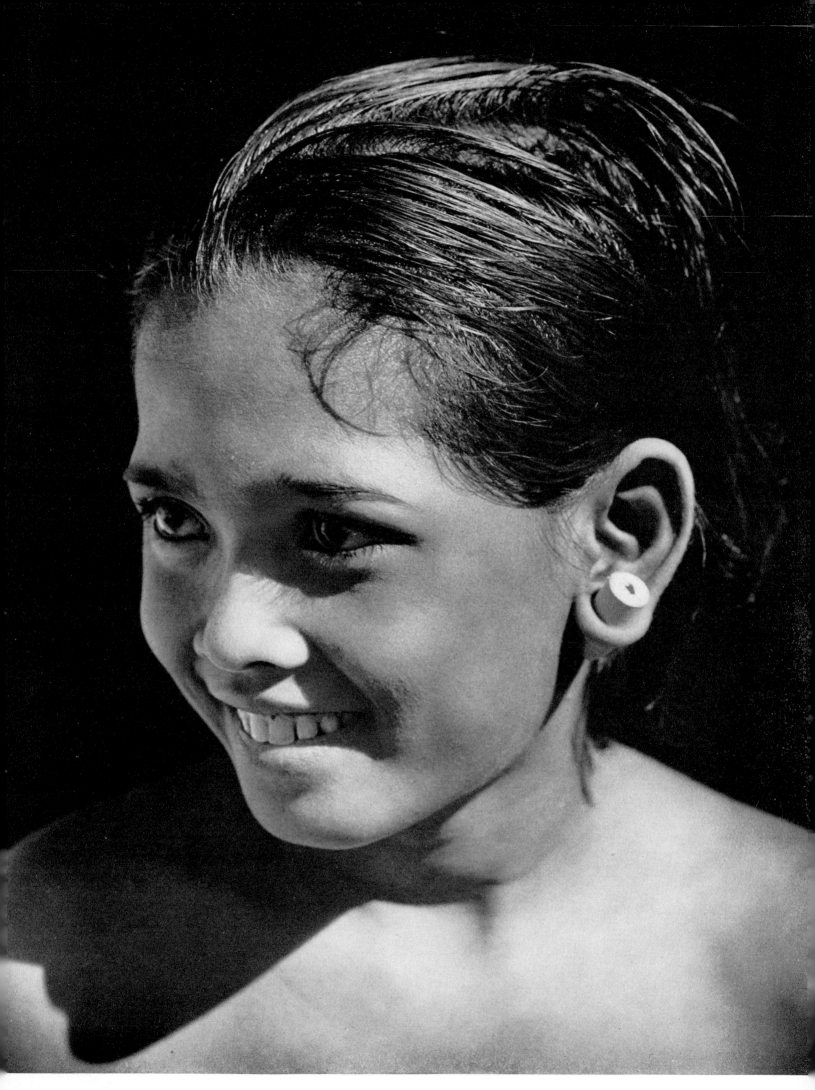

Child   31

Mountaineer

for their own. Modern education and Dutch schools taught by Javanese teachers have abetted the work of the missionaries. Children are not allowed in many schools unless they wear European shirts and blouses. The people are being taught shame. The radjas, and the ruling families, are, by their example, convincing the people of the superiority of European goods. But there are a few understanding officials, and it is possible that they may be able to curb the zeal of those men and women who would, perhaps unconsciously, destroy the happiness of others.

4

The religions of India clothe an ancient animism.

IN the remote mountain villages of Bali where neither the Hindu religion nor the influence of the princes has penetrated, there lives a race totally different from the ordinary Balinese in its religion and its mode of life. These villages are called Bali Aga, and their inhabitants consider themselves the descendants of the original inhabitants of Bali. Their religion is almost pure animism, similar to that of the early Indonesians, and the rules governing their lives are very strict.

Owing to the inaccessible locations of their villages and their poverty, these people have developed in their own way, and provide us with an illustration of what Bali might have been without its extraordinarily fertile soil and the religious and artistic stimulation of the Hindu-Javanese.

At the present time there are a number of so-called pure Bali Aga villages such as Sambiran in North Bali and others such as Tenganan and Asah near Karangasem, and Taro, above Oeboed, which have some of the aspects of ordinary Balinese life and differ widely from each other. There are many gradations between the pure Bali Aga and the typical Hindu-Balinese village. Though the Balinese are so closely bound together in the large concepts of their religion and their life, communalism has tended toward the individual development of each village in the smaller details, and it is difficult to discover what is normal.

Sambiran probably departs as much from this elusive norm as any village in Bali. It rises in tiers of thatched roofs against the rugged side of a mountain, and it can be reached only after a very steep climb from Djoelah on the coast, or over a precipitous trail from Kembangsari. For this reason, comparatively few white people bother to go to Sambiran. Its stone walls and streets seem strange after the eternal clay and mud of the rest of Bali. The main street ascending the mountain looks like the rocky course of a river bed.

The people of Sambiran seem far more primitive than those of the Hindu-Balinese villages. They are poorly dressed in dull cloths and are almost without ornament. They are also dirty and unkempt and exceedingly shy. They have little contact with other villages. A few people go to the markets in other districts, but the majority live and die in a very restricted area. They are not as intelligent as the ordinary Balinese, and they certainly do not have the same cheerful disposition. Both their religion and their life are more austere and lacking in much of the gay informality and colorful spectacle of the others. Their temples are rude affairs without sculpture, ornament, or any true architecture. There are no tall gates or intricately carved doors. Their orchestras do not compare with the magnificent gamelans of the Hindu-Balinese villages, and their instruments are primitive. Such dances as Baris are performed to satisfy religious demands; the fact of the performance, not the perfection of it, being important. There are great differences in religious practices, too. Cremation is the goal of the Hindu-Balinese, but in Sambiran, corpses are laid out on a bamboo platform in much the same manner adopted by the Parsees in India. After a specified period of time, if the corpse is still there, it is thrown into a ravine.

Tenganan, the much-publicized Bali Aga village near Karangasem, in reality falls into a special category. Unlike Sambiran, it is easily accessible and as a consequence has suffered a good many changes during the past ten years. Also unlike Sambiran, it is a very wealthy village owning many sawahs, and is celebrated for the richness of ornamentation and clothing of the people at its feasts and dances. The houses in Tenganan front on broad stone-paved streets which run parallel to each other. These form long narrow blocks and, where the houses are back to back, there are alleys in which the live stock is kept. In addition to the walls around each house compound, the entire village is walled.

Tenganan has many restrictions, such as the one against marriage outside of the village, and violation of any of them means expulsion from the village. So rigidly are these restrictions enforced that the numerous outcasts have formed a new village—more in the ordinary Balinese style—not far away.

Only certain dances may be done in Tenganan and those only at times prescribed by ritual. Redjang and Mendet are here performed beautifully, the costumes being particularly fine, including scarves of the famous "double ikat" which is made only in this one village.

Asah, between Tenganan and Karangasem, shows a further transition toward the Hindu-Balinese type. While in Sambiran the dead are left to be devoured by birds and animals and in Tenganan they are buried, in Asah they are cremated. There, I heard for the first time the gambang, a very ancient form of iron-keyed instrument used only at cremations. The costumes for the Redjang and Mendet are as elaborate as those of Tenganan. The laws of the village are less strict than in the pure Bali Aga villages, and there has been some foreign influence, as the Dutch have built a school there.

Taro, in the hills above Oeboed, and accessible only by a footpath from the Kintamani road, is also in transition from Bali Aga to the Hindu-Balinese. It has, or had in the spring of 1940, the finest Legong dancers in all Bali. The temple at Taro is a huge compound surrounded by an ornate wall with a massive gateway. Within the temple compound is an exceptionally fine council house with marvelous long straight timbers. This temple has several other large balés and squat meroes with deep palm-fibre thatch, out of which ferns grow. This is a distinct departure from the unpretentious Bali Aga temples. Taro also has many dances which are not found in the strict Bali Aga villages.

The Bali Aga are a remnant of the past carried into the present, and they are interesting for this reason, but only an anthropologist could long remain interested in these rather ordinary people when the colorful spectacle of the more advanced Hindu-Balinese civilization is so close. It is in the Hindu-Balinese villages that we find the colorful temple feasts, cremations, architecture, dances, and plays that we have come to associate with Bali. It is easier for us to consider the Hindu-Balinese as the Balinese people and the Bali Aga as a race apart, for this book is essentially about the former.

Though the Balinese have borrowed the gods of the ancient Hindu religion, they have invested them with many of the characteristics of their earlier Indonesian nature gods, and have in turn come to consider them as the deified ancestors of the Balinese race. Hinduism would have difficulty today in recognizing its spiritual child. The religion of the Balinese is, however, ideally suited to the volatile nature of the people, for it relies largely on pageantry and exoteric interpretation. It is infinitely appealing to the senses, for the innumerable feasts and ceremonies are all accompanied by music, dancing, drama and intricate offerings. Every temple in Bali has its temple feast on the anniversary of its birthday. There are in addition private feasts for such occasions as tooth filings, marriages, coming of age ceremonies, building a new house, or the harvesting of rice.

The Balinese calendar is a complicated affair which only a high priest can interpret. It is based on a year of two hundred and ten days in which weeks of one, two, three, four, five, six, seven, eight, nine, and ten days run consecutively. When certain days of certain weeks fall on the same day, that day may be lucky or unlucky. At the end of each two-hundred-and-ten-day year a great feast is held, which is called Galoengan. At this time the souls of the ancestors come down to earth to join in a great ten day feast which terminates on a day called Koeningan. During this holiday there is feasting over the entire island, and the holy Barongs, mythical lions, who at other times live in their enclosed balés in the temples, are allowed to roam over the countryside and dance for a few pennies where they will. During this time also the giant figures of the Barong Landoeng may be seen on the streets and dancing in the temple courtyards. These huge puppets, almost twice the height of a man, have peep-holes at the waist so that the actor may have a notion of what he is doing. The two chief figures are Djero Gede, a huge black man with white protruding upper teeth, and his companion Djero Loeh, an old woman with a white face and a wrinkled forehead. In the mountain villages there are never more than these two figures in the Barong Landoeng, but in the section around Denpasar there are several villages where the number has been increased to five. There is a male figure called Tjoepak and two female figures who might be sisters, so closely do they resemble one another. They wear yellow and red skirts and flowered blouses. Both have conventional white female masks with red lips and arched eyebrows. Their headdresses are similar to those worn by Legong dancers, and their long black hair streams forward over their shoulders. Tjoepak's face is a gross chocolate-colored mask with mouth ajar and teeth grimacing. It is crowned by an unruly mass of dark brown hair and over the left ear is a bunch of green foliage. In all cases, when the figures of the Barong Landoeng are not on the road, they are left in a balé, sitting in a circle as though about to begin a meal, and food is periodically set before them. I have seen such groups at Pemetjoetan, Pedangsandian, and Kedaton. Although the mask of Djero Loeh is usually round and has a protruding forehead, I saw one in a small town above Kloengkloeng which had a lean face with rather high cheek-bones and chiseled features.

Along with the Balinese year of two hundred and ten days there is the conventional solar year similar to our own, and every year at the spring equinox the Balinese celebrate a new year, which they call Njepi. The day before Njepi the island is cleansed of all devils by luring them to the temples with great feasts and then driving them out by the beating of koelkoels—hollow logs—and the shooting off of innumerable firecrackers. The day of Njepi itself is one of silence. In the stricter communities of South Bali and West Bali no one is allowed to go out of his house nor may any food be cooked. Even Europeans are forbidden to drive automobiles on the road, or are permitted to do so only upon payment of a heavy fine.

In the spring of 1940 both the great feasts of Galoengan and Njepi were celebrated within the space of a few weeks, and for the period of a month there was feasting and dancing everywhere. On the third day of Galoengan there was a feast at the temple of Batoekauh on the slopes of Goenoeng Batoekauh. All day long the women came from the surrounding countryside carrying huge offerings on their heads, up the steep wooded trails that lead to the temple. Pilgrims stopped at little shrines close to the main temple and came to the sacred springs for holy water. The entrance to the temple is through a wide gateway covered by green moss and lichen and tiny shreds of vegetation, so that it blends into the forest wall. It leads into a tremendous square with balés on either side and one just inside the gate for the gamelan, which was already playing. A small shrine off the entrance court was filled with pilgrims, and a pemangkoe—a low caste priest—in a white jacket and white headcloth scattered flowers as he prayed.

In the afternoon a second gamelan played within the inner court, which was clustered with tall meroes decorated with cloths and lamaks, and a dozen women danced a slow Mendet before one of the altars. People were continually arriving with offerings, and the temple was astir with their activities and the conflicting voices of the two gamelans which often played simultaneously. Later there was a very inept Kebyar danced by two small girls, which was followed by another Mendet, led by the oldest women with offerings on their heads, and followed by at least twenty-five women. They advanced slowly, thrusting their arms upward and at angles to their bodies, twisting, turning, stepping backward, and again advancing. These older women were neither beautiful nor were they fine dancers, but there was an air of intensity in their faces and a concentration in their attitude which made their dancing rhythmical and compelling. They danced several times around the outer courtyard in a single line. Presently the two leading women fell into a trance induced by the monotonous regularity of their movements and the rhythm of the music. A great crowd sat cross-legged on the ground or on the balés. The women danced on, the offerings on top of their heads never wavering. Their arms moved rhythmically. Green, red, blue, and salmon-pink costumes swirled and glided against a background of soft green, and golden flowers tossed on little springs in their hair. The music came to an abrupt end, and people started down the mountain trail; but the following day there was to be more feasting, more dancing, more music, and more offerings.

Two days later the great temple at Besakih held a feast in which all of the regents of the island and many of the Dutch government officials took part. The central court of the temple was littered with offerings, and in the surrounding balés were others. The three god seats held urns of gold and silver. Slender white and black and red banners, and white ceremonial umbrellas were on either side of the main altar. At the base of the god seats were two of the most elaborate offerings that I have ever seen. They were made entirely of colored sugar and contained little figures, tjilis, and lacy designs in red, yellow, and black. On either side were intricately-cut palm-leaf decorations and on top of each offering was a mass of frangipani flowers on slender upright sticks. There were few people in the temple, and there was none of the air of gaiety and warm human activity of the usual Balinese festival. Outside of the temple the regents and Dutch officials lunched to the music of gamelans. Later they sat in a balé while several pedandas—high priests— muttered their mantras, and the more humble pemangkoes carried offerings back and forth to the altar. One pedanda sat on a red cushion with his legs crossed. About him was grouped the paraphernalia of his office: his bell, a silver oil lamp with a gold top, and a golden censer. He wore a white cloth about his waist, and a narrow velvet strip was wrapped several times around his chest and carried over his left shoulder. Many strings of black, gold, blue, and crystal beads were criss-crossed over his shoulders and hung down below his waist. His tall, cylindrical miter was encrusted with gold and jewels, alternated in rows of gold and red, and culminating in a spear-shaped crystal. On either arm was a bracelet of gold and crystal beads and on the fingers of either hand were several heavy gold rings set with large stones. His face was lean, and deep furrows darted upward from between his eyes; his dark hair was gathered into a knot on top of his head beneath his miter, and wisps of dark mustache flowed from the corners of his upper lip. He rang his bell with his left hand, the fingernails of which were at least five inches long. With his right he scattered flower petals, sprinkled holy water and passed the censer back and forth in slow graceful movements before his face. All the while he concentrated with his eyes toward the end of his nose to induce trance. For a long time he continued to recite mantras and to move in another world.

During Galoengan the entire island is decorated with lamaks and pendjors. On the coast, northeast of Denpasar at Ketewel there were whole avenues of pendjors, their yellow palm-leaf pendants studded with red hibiscus blossoms. Outside of every gateway there were lamaks suspended from little shrines set on top of long bamboo poles, many of them ten or twelve feet high, and at Oeboed we found a huge triple lamak fully thirty feet long, hung from a platform with an upright bamboo fence and gateway, two spears, and a ceremonial umbrella. Women passed continually, carrying offerings of sweet cakes piled in artistic designs and topped with sprays of lacy bamboo, palm-leaf and red and orange flowers. At the approach of Koeningan, the day on which the souls of the ancestors again departed from the island, all of the pendjors, lamaks, and other offerings were renewed.

The feast of the temple on the island of Serangan just off the coast south of Denpasar was held on the day following Koeningan. All morning long people passed down the beach from Sanoer and Sindoe, and the white sails of boats carrying the pilgrims to the island glittered against the pale water and the deep blue of the sky. At low tide one may wade to the island, but when we crossed, the water was too deep, and the pilgrims had to wade out to the boats, holding high their ceremonial kains. The ripples caused by their passing sent back distorted reflections of magenta, green, and gold. It was a perfect day. Puffy cumulous clouds rose up on the horizon. Myriads of little sand crabs scuttled along the beach, avoiding the feet of the pilgrims. Later the sacred figures of the Barong Landoeng crossed to the island and danced in the temple courtyard, but much of the effect of the feast was lost, for many of the dandies from Denpasar came in European clothes or in soiled pajama jackets.

Far more interesting was the feast at Paksebali near Kloengkoeng, immediately preceding the new year. Here, women with offerings wound down the steep trails to the temple by the river, and small boys carried spears and ceremonial umbrellas atop long poles decorated with white cloths or gay, colored silk. Men followed carrying small litters, whose open fronts were curtained to protect the artjas, small wooden statues now inhabited by the deities. Meanwhile, in the village, eight young girls were being dressed to dance the Redjang. Their headdresses were high parabolas of orange-colored flowers topped by white flowers carved from the heart of palm. On either side of their foreheads were light palm discs with red flowers in the center. The orange flowers flowed down the back of the headdress, which was built up on an elaborate trellis bound into the hair, and the hair itself was covered by a thick foliage of green leaves. Ornamental woven kains, with soft-toned designs of green, brown, and magenta, trailed to the ground, and the breasts of the dancers were bound about with purple and blue cloth with gold-appliquéd designs. The gamelan was already playing in the temple, and the dancers, accompanied by older women, were taken into the inner court. Below, at the river temple, the artjas were being given their symbolical bath. People sat in solemn rows behind the gods, while a pemangkoe blessed them and scattered holy water and flowers before an altar. When the ceremony had been completed, the women climbed the steep trail to the upper temple. The booming of the gongs which accompanied the god carriers could be heard from the temple courtyard, and the explosion of firecrackers and the shouts of men shattered the orderly procedure of the feast. At the entrance to the temple, a solitary man appeared, stripped to a loin cloth and brandishing a kris. He came forward slowly, with glazed eyes and unsteady tread, and suddenly fell with tensed muscles upon his upturned kris. He pivoted slowly around, holding the handle of the kris on the ground and digging the upturned point into his breast. Several more men appeared brandishing krisses or walking in dazed circles; others suddenly finding life, jumped high into the air, shouting hoarsely; yet others whirled in a mad ecstasy, digging the krisses into their shoulders, into their breasts, into their cheeks. Then came the god carriers, also in a trance, the first pair staring wild-eyed at the exalted kris dancers. Somewhere in the distance the terrific explosion of firecrackers resounded, and as though a tension had been released, the men with the god carriers came forward, at first slowly, then in a mad rush, charging to the right and to the left. In a moment others were with them: six, eight, ten, twelve god carriers, madly twisting and turning, driving into the crowd, crashing against one another, stumbling, falling, being attacked by the kris dancers, ramming one another with all their might. Now the people in the crowd gave back, now they surged forward, or scrambled into a balé. The temple courtyard was a maelstrom of exploding firecrackers, dust, screaming people, crashes, and flashing krisses. Gradually the kris dancers subsided and were led away. The litters with their gods were returned to their places and the men, sprinkled with holy water, were left to recover in the inner temple. The gamelan played furiously, drums and gangsas, rejongs and trompongs, competing in a mad medley of sound. The huge gongs boomed out; the brown bodies of the players glistened with perspiration; the trompong player, in a magenta headcloth with three cigarettes protruding over his forhead, played as though entranced. Perspiration streamed down the brown shoulders of the drummers, and their hands flew. Red hibiscus behind the ears of each player were spots of color in the twilight. The mood was still one of savage exaltation, irreconcilable with the calm, slow movement of the Redjang. That night the dancers made offerings in the inner temple and then went home. Though they had not danced, they had cast a spot of beauty into an otherwise eerie scene.

This battle of the gods at Paksebali was not only spectacular; it was almost unique. All artjas receive a symbolical bath once a year, but in a very different way. The artjas from the great temple at Denpasar, after they had been imbued with the spirits of the gods whom they represent, were brought down to the beach at Koeta. They were carried on cushions on the heads of young girls and were shaded by ceremonial umbrellas, and were followed by many men with spears and banners, and women with offerings. Even the Poengawa, a high official, and a relative of the Regent, came. He rode on horseback, and as he was a large man and the Balinese horses are very small, he brought two extra horses with him. Several sheds, covered with palm-leaf thatch, had been set up on the beach on three sides of a square facing the sea, and on the fourth side were eight or ten temporary altars. Delicate bamboo poles bent gracefully over these altars on which the artjas were placed beneath the ceremonial umbrellas. A great feast of turtle meat, rice and other spiced foods was set out on leaf plates in a palm grove back from the beach, but the Regent and the Poengawa and their wives ate on the beach while a gamelan played. Later pemangkoes made offerings at the very edge of the water, and the inevitable lean and hungry dogs gobbled them up as soon as they touched the beach. In the early afternoon the Regent and the other high officials and their wives prayed beneath ceremonial umbrellas before the altars, after which the procession returned to Denpasar to the booming of gongs and the staccato explosion of firecrackers.

I saw a similar, though simpler, ceremony at Sanoer, but on this occasion five pemangkoes, three men and two women, danced on the beach in front of the artjas. Their hands performed delicate arabesques with smoking braziers. Back and forth they danced, weaving tangled trails of incense smoke until they had woven a spell about the gods, and had themselves fallen victims to their own enchantment. All the while the gamelan played monotonously, and the sound of the waves was no more than a whisper on the shore.

During Galoengan one occasionally comes across Ferris wheels twenty to thirty feet high which are revolved by man power. In some of the Bali Aga villages these wheels form a part of the religious ceremonial, but in South Bali the only apparent connection with religion is that the wheels are only used during Galoengan; the rest of the year they are covered with a framework of bamboo and palm matting. The supports for the wheels are made out of substantial tree trunks. The seats are enclosed in front and covered with a colorful cloth roof or awning and the woodwork is painted in blue, green and gold. These wheels attract large crowds of people, who pay a few kepengs and are whirled first one way and then the other to the accompaniment of screaming and laughter and the explosion of firecrackers, while dogs bark in bewilderment.

On the day preceding Njepi a high-roofed altar was set up in the great square of Kloengkoeng and was filled to overflowing with offerings to lure the demons. At dusk a yelling group of scantily clad men rushed at the altar, fighting and attempting to climb to the platform which contained the offerings, each man trying to prevent the others from getting there first. The whole structure swayed perilously and finally crashed to the ground, and in a few minutes the men had made off with the offerings of food and kepengs and had disappeared in the dusk. That evening a great fight with torches between rival bandjars was to have taken place, but though we waited until late in the night, nothing of consequence happened. Men with lighted torches prowled about the streets, but one faction was so far superior to the others that few ventured onto the central square. When they did, the torches of the stronger bandjar described parabolas of light in the darkness, and the others retired discreetly without offering any real opposition.

Balinese religion is everywhere concerned with the struggle between good and evil. The chief figures of this struggle are Barong, a mythical lion representing good, and Rangda, the fabulous widow witch, the incarnation of all dark and evil forces. The Balinese recognize that their world is not perfect, and that evil forces exist. In fact, they believe that these forces are so powerful that they must be propitiated. Both the Barong and the Rangda masks are, in themselves, so magically powerful that only persons of an especially strong character may wear them.

One afternoon I came by chance on a procession near Kapal. There was Barong with his ceremonial umbrellas, and Rangda being led by a pemangkoe on either side. Rangda, deep in a trance, walked blindly, and uttered weird grunts and moans. Several women were in trance also and flung themselves on the ground in utter abandon. Men picked them up and carried them into a little grove behind the temple, where they were laid against the boles of coconut trees or supported by other women. The day was already fading into an indistinct twilight, and the wavering light of a few torches cast eerie shadows among the trees; a fitting background for a weird scene. Fully a dozen women were lying about and weeping bitterly. I learned that these people had been to their temple of origin and that a priest in trance had been questioned as to the proper place to cut a new Rangda mask. During the ceremony many of the women, en rapport with the medium, had fallen into a trance, as had Rangda.

In the grove Rangda sat a little apart from the women, moaning and swaying to and fro. Suddenly she became violent and rushed about, clawing at men and women with her long-nailed white gloves. At first people paid no attention, but when she got out of hand, five men pinioned her arms and legs. She struggled, uttering a few unearthly yells, and then subsided into insensibility. Close to this spot a tree had been cut down, and offerings had been made to propitiate the spirit of the tree. Now a pemangkoe, a lean man with wavy white hair and a straggly beard, went among the women, sprinkling them with holy water. The people who were not in trance seemed little interested in the ones who were, except to restrain them in case of necessity. Later Rangda revived and danced to the music, but Barong remained quiet. This ceremony continued until dawn.

Balinese feasts are subject to so many delays that it is a wonder that they ever take place. A death in a village will automatically make a temple unclean, and the yearly feast may be postponed for months or never take place at all, though all of the preparations have already been made. The temple is closed and no one may enter. At such times it may even be impossible to perform a certain dance as the costumes may be kept in the temple and as no one is allowed to enter, they must remain there until the temple has been purified. But delays may be of a minor character. At a temple feast at Keramas, south of Gianjar, the feast was postponed for a day because at the last moment a priest decided that the sacred Barong had to be taken to his temple of origin, which was miles away at Semampan. The procession was led by girls with offerings in silver bowls on their heads, and by men with tall ceremonial umbrellas. Each of the girls wore a red blouse, the badge of some society. They were followed by men in white shirts and headdresses with check-ered black and white cloths about their waists, carrying red, white and blue flags and strange trifurcate spears. These men surrounded the Barong, which was led by two pe-mangkoes. In the temple at Semampan the Barong stretched out in front of the altar, his head in a mass of offerings of yellow palm-leaf and red hibiscus, his arched tail forming a golden question mark of darting flames and mirrors. The pemangkoes went among the crowd, distributing flowers and sprinkling the people with holy water. At intervals the chief pemangkoe faced the altar and prayed, and each person raised a flower to his fore-head between the middle fingers of either hand and then flung it from him. Following this ceremony, the procession returned to Keramas, wading through the streams, their progress punctuated by the inevitable explosion of firecrackers.

For days the women of Keramas had been preparing offerings for this feast. In balés inside of each compound, huge masses of fruit and pastries towered so high that they had to be supported from the roof. In temple feasts at Bonah and at Kedisan on Lake Batoer, I had already seen forests of offerings six to eight feet tall, set in rows in the temple courtyard. These were hollow tubes with light pastries fastened to the outer side. They could easily be carried by a man or supported on the head of a woman, and many times I have seen such offerings balanced on the heads of women half their height, who nevertheless walked at their usual pace and miraculously avoided the overhanging branches of trees. At Keramas, however, these offerings were of such solid fruits as bananas, djeroek, a large pink fruit somewhat like a grapefruit, and pineapples. They were supported at the four corners by tall bamboos and surmounted by yellow, red, and blue flowers. I watched eight men struggle to carry one of these offerings from a house to the temple, where it was placed with others on a platform raised three feet from the ground under a huge shed. The temple itself was elaborately decorated for the occasion. The small, sculptured raksasas were dressed in the sacred checkered black and white cloth and had white headcloths. The Barong had been replaced in his balé. Long hangings of silk were draped about the eaves of all the buildings. Before the principal altar, dedicated to the local deity, was a low platform covered with matting, on which were several silver bowls with offerings and two bottles with curious stoppers carved in the form of monkeys.

During the birthday feast of the temple at Kedisan, there were hundreds of offerings, all nearly identical. The base of each was an elaborately painted and gilded basket, per-haps twelve inches in diameter and eighteen inches high. Out of this, sprouted green palm leaves which enclosed a second basket decorated in the same manner as the first. Then there were brown, white, and red cakes of rice in broad stripes a foot high, and above these another row of cakes, white with black dots in the centers, topped by yet another of brown. The entire offering was surmounted by circular fringes of yellow palm-leaf. In the corners of the compound and in front of the meroes were other offerings nearly twice the height of the first, surmounted by ceremonial umbrellas and flowers. Baris spears with alternating black and white shafts stood before the principal meroe, which was also decorated with long bamboo poles with the leaves still on their upper sections.

At another temple feast at Blahbatoe, there were even taller and more elaborate offerings with stylized leaf designs running up each of their six sides. On the principal altar were complicated circles of pastry, colored sugar, and rice formed to resemble huge flowers, and in front of a balé were a dozen offerings set on bamboo poles split at the top to accom-modate the colored and gilded baskets, out of which sprang green leaves, pastry, and streamers of palm-leaf surmounted by a halo of feathery palm. There were also ceremonial umbrellas, spears, and flags. The balé was hung with a red cloth with a design of golden herons and leaves, and there was a cloth around the eaves having two broad white and red stripes running horizontally.

The Balinese, whenever possible, file their upper and lower front teeth, not into sharp points or down to the gums, but only enough to make them even. They believe that it is unlucky to be buried with teeth which in any way resemble those of animals, for in the next world they might be mistaken for animals and have to eat animal food. If they cannot afford the ceremony when they are young, it may be performed at other important periods during their lives, and in some cases the teeth of a corpse are filed before burial. I went to a tooth-filing ceremony at Gadji which preceded a wedding ceremony. When I arrived, a pemangkoe was already sitting on the ground before the house altar with an array of palm leaf offerings, flowers, bottles, and baskets in front of him. The boy and girl were dressed in ceremonial clothes and were being instructed in the ceremony by several old women. Firecrackers were set off before the altar, and palm offerings were sprinkled with holy water and tossed toward the altar by the pemangkoe. The boy was then led up to a balé which was richly decorated with cloths appliquéd with gold designs, and colorful woven silks. The balé was closed on two sides and open on the two others, and was almost completely filled by two huge beds. The boy was placed on one and was covered with a magnificent cloth, worked with silver thread. His mouth was propped open with a wedge and the filing begun with a coarse file which, by its looks, was originally intended for working metal. Meanwhile the boy's mother, a middle-aged woman with a beautiful face and black hair combed straight back and hanging in a full roll behind her head, sat beside him holding a child on her lap and occasionally inspecting the progress of the work. The gamelan played. An old man sang a fragmentary verse, and others joined in. People came and went. They seemed curious but not particularly sympathetic. No one objected to my standing with the family. People laughed and talked. The filing went on with occasional respites, when the boy would spit the filings into an empty coconut shell, and the family would inspect his teeth and discuss whether more needed to be taken off. I had been told that the person himself often made suggestions about the filing, but this boy kept very quiet and did not seem to enjoy the process, though he exhibited little emotion. When the work had been completed to everyone's satisfaction, the boy sat up, and a smoking brazier was placed at his feet, and more offerings were made. Then his place was taken by the girl. She had already had her teeth filed when she was younger, but they had not been made short enough, or had grown in again. At the first rasp of the file, she let out an involuntary cry, whereupon everyone laughed. So philosophical are these people about pain or death that any display of emotion is considered a weakness.

The marriage ceremony which took place shortly after the tooth-filing was a simple affair at which the bride and groom were given holy water to drink and several different foods to eat. A pemangkoe recited prayers before the house altar and wafted smoke from a brazier toward it with a palm fan. He then sprinkled holy water on the couple and poured some on their heads through a rice-steaming basket. Both the bride and the groom were continually prompted by old women. After the ceremonies, there was music and dancing during the afternoon and evening.

A girl comes of age at the end of her first menstruation and her family celebrates this event with feasting, music, dancing, and special ceremonies. I witnessed such a coming-of-age ceremony in Denpasar. While the girl was being dressed in ceremonial clothes, offerings were made at the house temple. A palm-leaf lattice had been set up over part of the courtyard, and the sunlight trickled through, mottling the faces of the people. An old man was reading passages from Wajang stories and discussing them with other men who sat about chewing sirih.

In another courtyard preparations were being made for a Wajang Koelit. When it is given at night the shadows of flat leather puppets are thrown against a white screen— viewed from the front, one sees the shadows; from the back, the puppets—but in this case the play was given in the daytime without a screen. The dalang, or story-teller, set his box of puppets behind a banana stalk which lay on the ground, and into the ends of which a stake had been driven and a line stretched between the two. Behind the story-teller was the orchestra, four men playing on metal-keyed instruments which have a scale unlike that of any other Balinese orchestra. Several children grouped themselves immediately in front of the impromptu stage. The dalang brought out first one puppet and then another and stuck them into the banana stalk, the good characters on the right side, and the evil ones on the left, and in the center a curious oval ornament which represents the story. These puppets, fantastic characters from the Ramayana and Mahabarata, are beautifully made of buffalo hide stamped out with iron dies into lacy designs and decorated with bright colors and gold leaf. Most characters are supported by a single stick and their arms are moved by two others. The dalang sat directly behind the center of his stage. On his left side was the box of puppets and between the toes of his right foot he held a wooden clapper which he knocked against the box to indicate to the orchestra a change of melody. After he had presented all of his characters, he took them down again, and the story began. As it progressed, more people gathered around. But now it

Dancer in Baris Démang 33

34   *Angkloeng*

Djanger at Koeta   35

36   *Kebyar at Bonah*

Dramatic Baris 37

Kris Dancers

Djoged Dancer   39

Girl in Child Baris

Legong at Taro

Pentjak

Rangda 43

44   Endé

Djoged Boem Boem 45

46   *Legong Dancer*

Ketjak   47

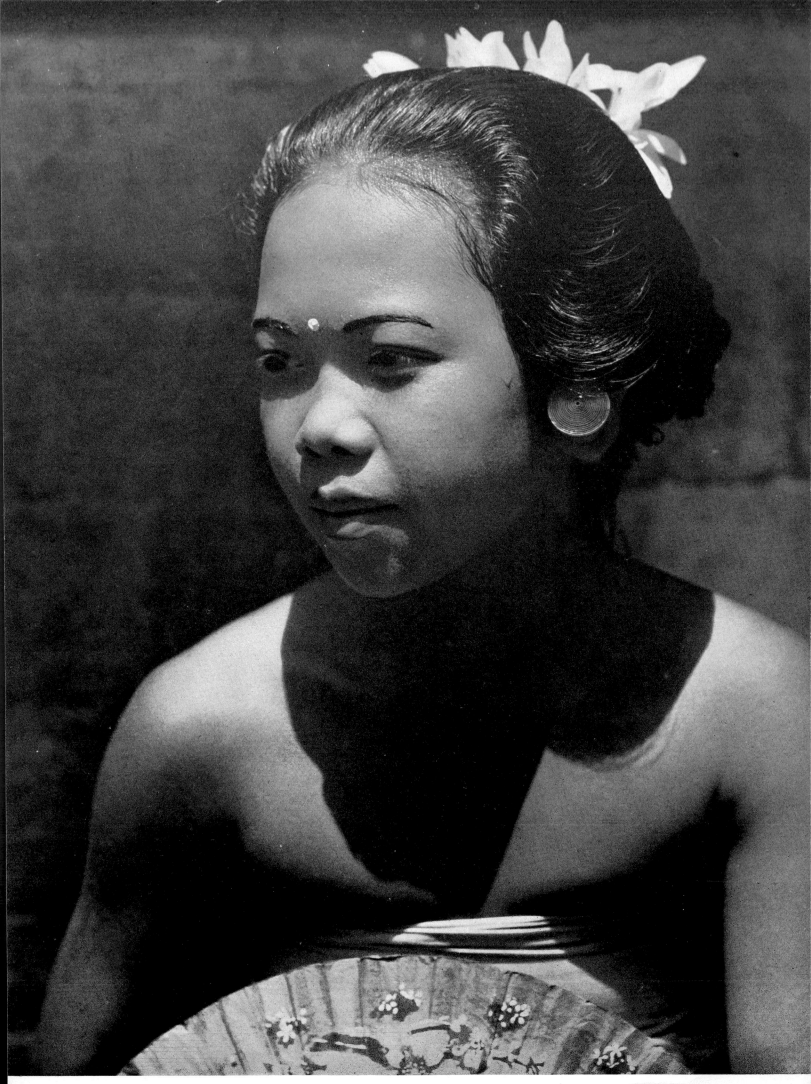

48   *Kebyar Dancer at Bonah*

was almost time for the ceremony to begin. Finally the girl came out, resplendent in gold headdress and ear plugs, and wearing a beautiful woven kain and a gold-appliquéd cloth wrapped around her breasts. She was brought out of the house on the shoulders of a man and placed in a litter which was then carried by eight men to a temple some distance away. Here she was set down before a shrine where she prayed and made offerings. During the procession and while she was at the temple, a very solemn expression never left her face, though everyone else took the matter lightly and enjoyed themselves as much as possible. This was quite in keeping with the Balinese character, for though their religion is of the utmost importance to the Balinese, they are unable to take its outward forms too seriously, no matter what the occasion. The girl, herself, was passing through a new experience, and she was a little bewildered, but had the ceremony concerned someone else, she would not have given its deeper significance a second thought, for the Balinese are by nature extroverts.

The Balinese believe in reincarnation, and consequently spend very little time mourning for the dead, but they believe that unless the body of a dead person is cremated, his soul will haunt the neighborhood of his body and trouble his relatives. Cremation has been practiced in Bali since the twelfth or thirteenth century by those Balinese who were affected by Hindu culture, which is to say, at least nine out of ten. Cremations are one of the most colorful aspects of Balinese religion, and because of their importance they are also the greatest occasions for feasting and celebration. When a man dies, he is buried. After forty-two days the corpse may be dug up and cremated, but it seldom occurs that there is an auspicious date immediately following the forty-two day period, or that the family has been able to raise sufficient money to provide a fitting cremation, for cremations are costly affairs. Great sums of money are spent for the huge cremation towers, and the high priests must be paid well for their services; the family must also provide food, music, and dancing for hundreds of guests. But it is important that the soul should have as elaborate a send-off as possible, and people often save for years in anticipation of their own cremation. If there is not enough money at the time of their death, it may be two, five, ten, or even twenty years before they are cremated, but a son seldom fails to have his father or mother cremated eventually, though he may have to sacrifice greatly to accomplish this. If a body has been buried for so long that it is impossible to find any of the bones, the person is then cremated in effigy. Cremation is almost universal among the Hindu-Balinese, but people who have died of leprosy, or have been convicted of certain crimes, may not be cremated.

I saw my first cremation not long after I came to Bali. It was one in which I took a personal interest because the cremation towers and animals grew before my eyes every day as I drove from Denpasar to Koeta. There were three cremation animals, two cows and a bull, which, from blocks of wood, became gorgeous yellow and orange beasts with gold horns, red eyes with black pupils, and long wisps of green grass at the ends of their tails. The cremation towers were built under a tall shed of palm matting. There was one with seven pagoda-like roofs denoting that it was for a goesti, a person of the third caste. It had a solid box-like base with four pillars extending upwards from the corners to the roof. The base of the largest of the three towers was covered with a red paper with center inserts of a blue background on each side; the whole covered by white paper cut into an intricate design. The supporting columns were covered with a flowered paper, and the seven roofs were white with elaborate paper ornaments flowing down each hip. The tower was supported on strong bamboo poles, criss-crossed and extending on all sides beyond the base.

On the day of the cremation a great crowd was already surging about in the road when we arrived, and within the house compound the family were completing the last rites. There was a great confusion of people coming and going. On the wall of a balé was the head of a carabao resting in a basket at the end of an upright pole. Many offerings were brought to the balé and placed with many others. Some of the offerings had been there for several days, and the atmosphere was heavy with the smell of decaying food. Gaunt dogs prowled about, and periodically firecrackers were exploded. Outside, laughing, yelling men were carrying the cremation animals up and down the road, shouting, struggling, falling into the ditches, and charging at the men carrying other animals. This was to mislead the evil spirits. When everything was ready, the corpses, wound in trailing white sheets, were brought out over the wall of the compound instead of through the gate, and with much confusion were placed in their respective towers. Fifty to seventy-five men, with their kains girt up to form loin cloths, took up each tower and started toward the cremation ground. In a moment they surged back again, past the house, in the wrong direction. Great clouds of dust from the road rose into the air, and the sound of exploding firecrackers was deafening. At times the towers swayed perilously, but they were always righted just in time. A close relative of the dead person rode on each tower, high up where the winding sheet of the corpse fluttered from a platform, and each tower was guided by a long rope held in the hands of relatives. The procession was led by Baris dancers, their peaked hats, black and white checked costumes, and long spears adding immeasurably to the effect. At the cremation grounds crowds had collected, the inevitable food stands had been set up, and a gamelan was already playing. There were two long rows of unornamented boxes on stands, which contained the bodies of poor people, who, by joining the retinue of the departing soul of the goesti, had the advantage of the prayers and ceremonies which they could not otherwise afford. The soul of the goesti, in turn, gained prestige by being accompanied by so many people into heaven. The cremation animals were placed on the ground, and the crowd surged around and about. At one end of the ground two of the tall towers were partially dismantled. The two yellow cows were placed on the lower platform of the largest tower, and the orange-colored bull was placed in a similar manner on the smaller tower. The backs of the cremation animals were lifted off, and the corpses placed inside. Relatives immediately climbed onto the platforms to have their last words with the dead. Offerings were heaped high on the corpses and beneath the animals.

Meanwhile, the Baris was taking place; two lines of men with spears advanced slowly, raising their knees high and at an angle to the body. They retreated and advanced again, their spears at right angles to the ground and then pointed obliquely toward it. Presently these spears were placed on the ground, and the men went forward, posturing slowly. People formed a hollow square about the dancers. They clustered on a small hillock overlooking the ground. They climbed over the animals, and the long line of sarcophagi of the poor people was a mass of activity. Two tall trees rose up at one edge of the clearing and cast lengthening shadows upon the cremation ground. The Baris dancers completed their slow ceremonial dance and were each given a few kepengs that had formed a part of the offerings. At last the relatives stepped down from the towers, and a man with a torch set fire to the many offerings beneath the animals. Instantly flames and smoke sprang up, and the belly of the nearest animal became a glowing framework. A black, red-rimmed stain spread over the side of the animal. Smoke came from the long line of coffins. Relatives poked tentatively with long sticks so that the fire would burn more fiercely. The tower of the goesti was a mass of flames, and presently the roof caught, and a sheet of fire vied with the setting sun. One by one the animals collapsed under the stark, charred framework of the towers. People started slowly for home, and only a few relatives were left to make sure that the bodies were completely burned and to collect the ashes.

The most magnificent cremation in many years was that of the Radja of Tabanan in November 1939. The Radja had been dead for more than a year, but the priests had hesitated for a long time before selecting a day auspicious enough for so important a person. When we came to the great square in Tabanan, the crowd was so large that it was impossible to get near the cremation tower, which stood just outside the poeri, or palace. But from a distance we could admire its eleven glittering roofs, brilliant against a background of dark green trees. Great multi-colored wings sprang from either side of a Bhoma head and rose fully twenty feet at the back of the tower. The front was a solid mass of gold and mirrors.

A long procession had already formed, and at the head of it was the cremation animal, a magnificent winged lion. A little behind, on a golden chair carried by eight men, rode the widow of the Radja. The explosion of enough firecrackers to scare every demon from the island announced that the corpse of the Radja was being brought from the poeri to the cremation tower. The corpse was to be carried over a bridge thirty feet high, constructed of bamboo and hung with lacy fragments of palm-leaf, in order to reach the high superstructure of the tower. On this bridge a great fight took place; the long white winding sheets of the corpse being fought over so furiously by two opposing groups of men that, for a moment, the bridge threatened to collapse into the crowd below.

The great hill on which the cremations take place was more than a mile away, and we hastened there so that we would be ahead of the procession. It was already overrun with thousands of people in brilliant magenta and green, orange and brown sarongs, their brown bodies blending with the soft green of the hillside. So colorful was the scene that only the beating of the koelkoel and the sound of bursting firecrackers recalled to me that the procession must have started. In a little while, the tall ceremonial umbrellas and the cremation tower became visible through the trees. The men came on with scarcely a halt—evidently there was no longer any need to confuse the evil spirits. The procession turned off the road and started up the hill, and now a spectacle of the utmost magnificence streamed slowly past. Hundreds of men and women in gaily colored clothes came first, some carrying ceremonial umbrellas; then came a tall slender peach-colored banner like those used in temple feasts, or in certain dances, carried by a man who preceded the cremation animal. There followed the animal itself under two deep blue umbrellas topped by golden points and ornamented with gold. The animal was carried by fifty men with white cloths wound around their heads, flowers tucked into them. Their brown bodies glistened with perspiration, their muscles strained, and above them sprang up the glittering figure of the winged lion. He was a dark red, and his tall neck arched and ended in a fierce face with mouth open, and tongue extended. Two huge wings of gold with magenta and green feathers rose from his shoulders, and golden flames sprang from his curled tail and bristling mane. He stood in a field of magenta, blue, green, and gold. The sun shone full in the face of this winged beast, who seemed to glow with an inner light. Behind came the huge cremation tower carried by more than a hundred men. From a distance the base and wings shone in the sunlight. The roof rose tier after tier against a solid background of soft green bamboo and terraced rice-fields, and from each roof hung a silken curtain, yellow, green, red, purple, orange, pink, and above them all a golden linga pointed toward the sky. Dark, brooding clouds hung in the east, and the resplendent lion and the tower stood out as though they had been spotlighted.

The procession continued up the hill, shouting. The huge Bhoma head; the wings, pale blue, green, yellow, and red, outlined with black; the long winding sheets of the corpse stringing out for forty or fifty feet; and the mirrored sides of the tower all flashed in the sun. The tower was carried around the field three times and then brought to rest next to the bridge which led down to a platform surrounded by a red and gold wall like that of a temple. In front was a split gateway, also red and gold, outlined with black and with white roofs. Over the platform was a tall roof of white cloth supported by four slender white columns with a thin red line running along their outer edges. The corpse was carried down the bridge, handed from one person to another and placed in the winged lion.

Facing the cremation platform was another platform perhaps ten feet square, raised high from the ground and covered with a thatched roof. On it sat four priests and a priestess, praying, raising their hands, palms pressed together, their extended fingers holding flower petals. As they murmured the sacred mantras, they pressed the petals to their forehead and tossed them away. A gamelan played at intervals, and the huge crowd prepared to wait while relatives, friends, and officials passed in a long line in front of the cremation animal. Costly silks, kains, and irreplaceable woven cloths were placed on the corpse. Then came a group of people carrying earthen jars of holy water. A priest and a near relative took them, as the people filed up, and poured water over the corpse, then dashed the jars to the ground where they shattered into fragments.

Now the clouds in the sky grew darker and cast a gloom over the celebration. The gamelan played, the priests still prayed. As though loath to burn so much magnificence, people came in an endless procession. The silken offerings, piled high on top of the animal, and beneath him, streamed from his head and his wings. At last the walls about the platform were taken down. A torch, lighted from a sacred fire, was touched to a trailing scarf, and the flames ran up it eagerly, and in a moment all was ablaze, even the sacred umbrellas.

Tongues of flame licked at the dark sky from which a few drops of rain fell. A passing shower hollowed out small craters in the light dust. The water hissed as it smote at the flame. The people crowded forward eagerly. Men poked at the fire and the flames leaped higher. The bright soul of the Radja was escaping to another life. Finally the lion lurched forward and crashed on his face. The wings crumpled. For a little while it stood, up ended, and then the back legs gave slowly away and it became one with the flaming pyre, now only a beacon in the darkness.

I saw one very curious cremation at Sindoe which followed five days after the death of a pedanda. This in itself was unusual, as forty-two days generally must elapse before a body may be cremated. But high priests may not be buried, and as a particularly auspicious date followed immediately upon the pedanda's death, it was decided to cremate him immediately. This cremation was made even more strange by the apparent telescoping of the cremation ceremonies with the moekoer ceremonies, which usually follow forty-two days later, so that instead of months or even years elapsing after his death, his body had been cremated and his soul liberated and consecrated within the brief period of five days. This left such a short time for preparation that the entire bandjar was a beehive of activity. The cremation tower and cremation animal appeared as if by magic. The corpse was laid out in a balé within the house compound, and was attended day and night by relatives. Orchestras played at intervals, and people came and went with offerings. No effort was made to embalm the body, and by the end of the fourth day, the atmosphere in the neighborhood of the balé was unbearable. On the day of the cremation, the finished bull, in which the pedanda was to be cremated, stood in the outer courtyard. This bull was a terra-cotta color and had long golden horns and a golden flower in each ear. Around his neck hung an orange sash partially covering an intricate breast ornament of tooled leather covered with gold leaf. He had great round eyes with concentric circles of white, black, and red, and in the center, black pupils. His eyelashes and lips were a crinkled mass of gold leaf, and his eyebrows were upright and delicately curved pieces of gold, which shaded his protuberant eyes. In his mouth was a realistic bundle of grass. The cremation tower of a pedanda represents the seat of the Sun God. This one was no more than ten feet high and rudely built, because there had been so little time in which to prepare.

By the afternoon of the fifth day the preparations had been completed, and the procession started down the short road to the beach, accompanied by the usual shouting and the explosions of the firecrackers. The men carrying the bull came first, followed closely by the cremation tower, the corpse slanting forward and trailing its winding sheets. When they came to the beach, the men carrying the tower proceeded far out into knee-deep water, splashing, stumbling, and yelling. Finally the tower was brought back and set down close to the palm-lined beach, and the body was lifted into the cremation animal, which was raised onto a platform of kindling. A procession of women and girls, carrying offerings and effigies of the gods on their heads, then came down the avenue, shaded by ceremonial umbrellas in the hands of men. The offerings were placed on the beach, and a priest prayed over them. The good-byes to the departing soul of the pedanda were brief, and in a short time the cremation animal dissolved in a mass of flames, the dry wood which formed the base of the fire burning fiercely. Presently men came down to the water's edge bearing small bundles of ashes bound in white cloth. They stripped and plunged into the water, where they engaged in a furious battle for the bundles, which were thrown high into the air, only to be fought over by another group. A little apart, further up the beach, the women stripped off their clothes and bathed separately. Finally a canoe set out with the remaining ashes, which were to be cast into the water, far from land so that there would be no possibility of them being washed ashore.

5

A land of pure music and heroic drama. It is a dancer's dream come true.

THE dance and drama of Bali have their roots in India and many of the stories come directly from the Ramayana and the Mahabarata. It has been suggested that the dance originated with the intricate and beautiful hand movements of the Indian priests during their prayers; indeed such dances as the Kebyar, which is done entirely in a sitting position, the movement being limited to the hands, arms and torso, could be considered as an evolution from such a source. But the urge to dance is almost universal, and it is more probable that the Balinese dance originated in this natural impulse for self-expression. People of primitive societies, having no complicated mental problems to solve, find expression in physical ways, and the dance satisfies their need for action. It may also induce a rhythm either warlike, mystical, or erotic.

In Bali there are stylized combats such as Endé and Pentjak which undoubtedly started as martial exercises. Endé is actual combat with rattan staves, while Pentjak is a series of stylized poses either with or without weapons, emphasis being placed on the graceful transition from one pose to another. Though Pentjak may now be considered a dance because there is little feeling of actual combat, Endé is only allied to the dance form because its movement is rhythmical.

Baris was originally a dedication of the warrior and his weapon to the temple. Today there are many different types of Baris, varying from the primitive Baris of the Bali Aga villages to the highly developed Dramatic Baris with its spectacular combats between rival princes.

NOTE: The dancer is often called by the same name as the dance. For the sake of clarity the names of dances have been spelled with a capital letter, the dancer with a small letter: thus a *legong* is a dancer in the *Legong*, a *djoged* a dancer in the *Djoged*.

There are dances such as Djoged and Gandroeng which appear to be erotic, and others like Djanger which are partly social, yet the Djoged, Gandroeng, and Djanger borrow from older dance forms, the significance of which has been carried over.

Religion, which is inseparable from any phase of Balinese life, is the chief inspiration for the dance. Such dances as Gabor and Redjang are a dedication of the bodies of the dancers to the gods, and in Mendet, offerings of flowers and intricately cut palm-leaf are carried in a slow dance to the altar. Sanghyang is performed by young girls without previous training who dance perfectly once they have become possessed by the gods: it is an exorcism of evil spirits in the village. Ketjak, a dramatic dance performed by more than a hundred men, is an outgrowth of the vocal accompaniment to the Sanghyang. Barong has great religious significance, as it portrays the everlasting struggle between good and evil, and it must be performed in the village on certain occasions. In South Bali almost every bandjar has its Barong and, at certain seasons, these extraordinary beasts with their retinues roam the countryside at will.

Legong, though a dance, is dramatic and tells a story. It is very popular at feasts of all kinds, and legongs are often the darlings of a village. Kebyar, a recent development, is almost entirely a musical interpretation.

Balinese drama is invested with certain stock characters and situations which reappear endlessly. Consequently the emphasis is always placed on performance, as the plot is already well known to everyone. The most important of these characters are Barong, already mentioned, representing good, and Rangda, a witch, personifying evil. Rangda literally translated means widow, and one story identifies Rangda with the mother of the famous Balinese king, Erlangga, who ruled in East Java in the eleventh century. She was exiled to the forest by Erlangga's father, then ruler of Bali, because she practiced witchcraft. After his death she attempted to kill Erlangga and destroy his kingdom, but was bested by Mpu Bharada, a holy man, who was Erlangga's teacher. Widows were looked down upon at that time because most high caste women preferred to be burned with their husbands. Erlangga's mother was not only a widow, but practiced black magic. As a result, she became a symbol of evil.

Throughout Balinese dance, drama, literature, and religion is the ever-recurring struggle of good against evil, the high against the low, the right against the left, Barong against Rangda. Both the Barong and Rangda masks are very holy and are kept in a special building in the temple. A new mask must be properly blessed before it is used, and appropriate ceremonies are also necessary before each performance.

Actors in Bali are "possessed" by their roles, which are so familiar to them that for a time they lose their own identity. They frequently fall into a trance and thereafter act without volition. There have been several cases of injury, and one death of a Rangda attacked by entranced kris dancers in a Barong play.

Other characters of the Balinese stage include princes, patihs, or prime ministers, servants, who are always clowns, princesses, and ladies' maids.

The ordinary play is introduced slowly by the appearance of a patih, or a servant, or both, who paves the way for the prince. Stock characters also play stock parts, that is to say, a prince of a certain type always speaks and acts and even walks in a prescribed way, and his patih always follows a set style of his own. Only the clowns are allowed a certain amount of invention, and it is they who are the most interesting to the ordinary person. Princes and such high characters speak in Kawi, the classical language of Java and Bali, which is unintelligible to all but a few highly educated people; the clowns discuss the prince and princely sayings in the vernacular.

It may seem strange that the Balinese peasant thoroughly enjoys a theater when he can understand only half of what is said, but, to begin with, he is completely at home with the characters of his stage. He has known them from earliest childhood, when at his mother's breast he has watched the plays unfold and listened to the music. All parts are not only distinguishable by costume, makeup, or mask, but also by type of movement, tone of voice, and even by the music which announces the characters. The stories, learned by constant repetition, soon become so familiar that it does not matter where they are begun or left off, nor is it necessary to understand the words.

For all of these reasons, the attitude of the Balinese audience differs greatly from that of our own. The circumstances governing performances also are very different. Dances and dramatic performances are given primarily to fulfill religious demands, but they also form a large part of the entertainment of the people, and they are therefore largely attended. There is no such thing in Bali as a performance for which admission is charged, and at all performances everyone is welcome. In this way rich and poor alike have an opportunity of seeing innumerable plays and dances. They also share equally in the performance, for the only qualification is the talent of the performer. Caste distinctions are abandoned on the stage, and a high caste man thinks nothing of sitting at a lower level in an orchestra than his low caste partners. The Anak Agoeng of Soekawati, a man of very high rank, often played the part of a clown, which he did superbly, while a peasant played the part of a prince.

The audience furthermore has no obligations to the actors or to those providing the entertainment, as the performance has been provided either in the religious interests of the community or by an individual to celebrate a birthday, a wedding, a tooth-filing, the completion of a house, or some other necessary ceremony, none of which are complete without music, dancing, or a play. As the spectators are free to come and go as they wish without fear of offending their hosts or the performers, the only indications of the worth of a performance are the size of the crowd, the length of time that the people remain, and the amount of attention paid to the actors or dancers. During the less interesting parts, the people in the audience talk to their friends and walk back and forth across the stage, which is generally no more than a hollow square of which the orchestra forms one side and the audience the other three. Children and dogs wander about at will, and at the conclusion there is no clapping or approval of any sort; the people simply vanish into the night.

As with so many other things in Bali, the astonishing progress of the Balinese theater is due to the effort of the entire community. All dances and plays are performed by members of societies which originated either in answer to religious demands, for recreation, or in a spirit of competition with other villages. Of course, love of the arts is born into these people, and, once initiated, it has become a large part of the environment of succeeding generations, and thus the original impulse has been multiplied many times.

There are societies for each dance or orchestra, and each play. The function of the society is to select the most promising players, to engage a teacher, and to make the arrangements for all rehearsals and performances. The society usually owns the costumes or the instruments, which are very often expensive, and cares for any money that may be received. Money paid to a society is almost never distributed among the members, but is instead put into the treasury to buy new costumes or instruments, or to pay a celebrated teacher for further instruction. Performances of a village orchestra or dance society are never paid for when they are given in the village. They are considered to be a proper contribution to the life of the community and a return for the time and money spent in training the players; even an individual within the village pays only a nominal fee to the society, but another village will often pay as much as forty or fifty guilders to a particularly fine orchestra even though they may have one of their own which would fulfill their religious requirements. This is an undeniable demonstration of the Balinese love of music and artistry. Competitions are held between the villages in different sections of the island to select the finest gamelan, and rivalry is very keen.

The length of life of these societies depends on the demand, the interest, the people available, and the fashion of the day. Certain dances such as Sanghyang may be required only in times of great misfortune in a community, in which case dancers are trained and then disbanded after the emergency has passed. Others like Barong or Legong are in periodic demand and most villages keep such societies constantly alive, but it may so happen that the small girls who dance Legong become too old and no others of sufficient talent are available, or that the actor who plays Barong, an exacting role, dies. In such cases a Legong or Barong must be engaged from another village. Fashion plays its part even in Bali, and a dance that may one year be very popular, may a few years hence be all but extinct. This is true of Djanger, which originated in North Bali after a Malay Operetta had visited there. It swept the island ten years ago, but it is difficult to find a good Djanger today. Ketjak, also, has disappeared except in a few isolated communities.

The Balinese have borrowed indiscriminately from all sources for their arts. The North Balinese, who have had longer contact with the outside world, have always been the greatest innovators, while the people of South Bali have refined whatever came to their attention. They have discarded much, and transformed what remained into something original and unmistakably Balinese. The Balinese are the rare people who, instead of becoming smug, have been willing to try anything new for fear that they might be missing some very powerful magic; and the yet more rare people who, having borrowed profusely, have still been able to retain their own individuality.

It is almost impossible to separate dance from drama, or either from music, and all three are inextricably bound up with religion. In spite of this, each is highly specialized.

In Bali there are orchestras for almost every occasion. The full kebyar gong is comparable to our symphony orchestra, whereas the small orchestras which accompany processions may contain only a few gongs and cymbals.

One of the few orchestras which is never accompanied by dancing is the angkloeng. This orchestra takes its name from four curious instruments which, when shaken, produce one note of a four-note scale. Other instruments in this orchestra include small drums, medium-sized gongs, and instruments with four metal keys struck with a padded stick held in the right hand, the keys being dampened with the left hand. The very elaborate angkloeng orchestra at Tjoelik in East Bali also has a large instrument similar to a xylophone, which is set on a stand, high in front and low in the back, so that it rests in the lap of the player, who squats on the ground. This instrument is most elaborately carved and painted in red, yellow, black, and gold. Nagas, mythical serpents, wind about either side and raise their heads high above the front. Nagas also wriggle down the sides of the ang-kloengs, their gold-crowned heads doubling back upon their bodies. These angkloengs, probably the most elaborate in Bali, have a hollow bamboo base into which four black palm stakes, a half-inch in diameter and three feet high, are inserted at regular intervals. The stakes culminate in golden spear-tips with red, white, and black tassels. Between each pair of stakes is hung a hollow bamboo, the three being graduated in height from two feet to no more than eight inches and being suspended so that they swing loosely in slots in the base. There is also a curious instrument consisting of two knobbed gongs, one at either end of a wooden support, the whole like a huge dumbbell. This is held on the knees of the player and is hit with two padded sticks, one held in either hand. Not so spectacu-lar as the kebyar gong, angkloeng music can be compared with our chamber music.

There are orchestras for cremations and temple feasts which require no dance accom-paniment, and both the kebyar gong, and the important pelegongan orchestra, which accompanies the Legong, Barong, and Tjalonarang performances, play long introductory pieces and intermission music. But no orchestra is more curious than the Genggong, which is a hodgepodge of miscellaneous instruments, the principal one from which the orchestra takes its name, resembling a jew's-harp. The Genggong at Taman was made up of nineteen players, each wearing a black headdress into which a scarlet hibiscus flower had been stuck. The Genggong players formed two lines of four players each, facing one another. At the far end was the leader who also played the genggong, and behind him were other players with a variety of curious instruments: a huge toad formed the base of a tjeng-tjeng—cymbals; two frogs held suspended between them two glass cylinders which were hit with sticks with iron discs at their ends; there were also small drums no more than eight inches in diameter and eighteen inches long; long flutes extending to the ground, and others no larger than a conductor's baton. The genggong is made of an eight-inch piece of black palm to which a vibrating string is attached, and a large leaf-shaped tortoise-shell vibrator which is held over the mouth. It is held in the left hand of the player. The vibrating string, attached to which is a foot-long wand pointed and gilded, is actuated by the right hand. The music of the Genggong at Taman was elfin in charac-ter. The leader danced an accompaniment from a sitting position. This old man had a grand, intense face, somewhat Caucasian in character. He swayed gently from side to side on crossed legs, sometimes holding the tortoise-shell resonator of the Genggong close to his face and at other times discarding it entirely for expressive gestures of his hands.

The two lines of men playing the Genggongs swayed forward, then away from one another. The entire performance was of the utmost charm, and the music had a peculiar fascination, despite its strange character.

Balinese music is pure music. It has a tremendous vitality, a compelling rhythm, and is highly syncopated. The instruments in the various types of gamelans are chiefly percussive, and it is almost impossible for the unaccustomed western ear to solve the complicated polyphony of a kebyar gong. There is no written score, and the gamelan is led by the drummers, who are usually the most accomplished musicians. New pieces are constantly developed from old, and no two orchestras play a composition in exactly the same way. Love of mysic is universal in Bali, and every Balinese man can play at least one instrument. Each village supports as many orchestras as it can afford. All of the metal and bamboo-keyed instruments are made on the island, but the large gongs have to be imported from Java.

The usually frugal Balinese spend huge sums on their musical instruments, but the most astonishing thing about their music is the fact that it is entirely supported by a race of small farmers who have had little or no formal education and to whom music is a means of relaxation. Memorizing some of the longer compositions, which are pure tonal patterns, is no inconsiderable feat, but tiny children absorb the very essence of the music from between the knees of their fathers, and by the time they are six or seven, many of them are already accomplished musicians.

In the large orchestras there are two drums, one male and the other female, long truncated cones of wood covered on the ends with buffalo hide, the male being slightly the larger. These drums are held in the laps of the players, sitting cross-legged, and are struck on both ends with the hands and with padded sticks. The physical effort expended in playing one of these great drums, three and a half to four feet long, is tremendous, yet the men play on for hours, delicately strumming with their fingers, hitting with the full flat of their hand, climaxing a passage by a lightning crescendo of furious sound. The majority of the instruments in most types of orchestras have flat metal or bamboo keys. There are also large and small gongs and tjeng-tjengs, cymbals, two of which are attached to a permanent support and the other two held in the hands and clashed together. In the kebyar gong there are two instruments, the trompong and the reyong, which consist of rows of knobbed gongs supported on a horizontal framework. The trompong, of ten gongs, is played by a single musician, while the reyong, generally of thirteen gongs, is played by four musicians, who sit behind it. In addition to these instruments there are, in some orchestras, several different types of flutes, and the reybab, a violin borrowed from the Arabians. There are also a few primitive instruments such as the genggong, and various percussive instruments made from bottles, or tubes of glass.

The Balinese have an orchestra for every occasion and most employ a five-note scale. However, the angkloeng, an ancient type, has a four-note scale, and there are others in which a seven-note scale is still used. There are special orchestras for temple feasts, for cremations, and for processions, as well as innumerable types for different dances. All of this makes for variety and increased interest. Balinese music, in spite of its involved counterpoint and its highly syncopated nature, is understandable to the western ear. Its strong rhythmic undercurrent gives it a cohesion that is lacking in almost all other oriental music with the possible exception of that of India.

It was inevitable that some of the first music that I heard, and some of the first dances that I saw after I came to Bali, should be at the Bali Hotel. These are, in fact, the only dances that many tourists do see. The KPM, the Dutch shipping company which owns the Bali Hotel, controls the shipping to the island, and monopolizes the tourist trade, has done much, perhaps too much, to make the dances and music both dramatic and interesting. A beautiful pavilion has been built in the hotel courtyard, and at least one night each week dances are given for both the townspeople and the tourists. When I first saw these performances, I was interested in the sheer virtuosity of some of the music and dances. But I had already seen many stage shows more elaborately presented, so I was not impressed. This was not very different from Broadway or Hollywood. Later, after I had seen dozens of performances in the different towns throughout Bali, I understood why these performances at the Bali Hotel, though by many of the same gamelans and dancers, appeared to lack something essential. The stage setting of the KPM is too overpowering and in some ways too artificial an atmosphere for Balinese dance and music. But most important of all, the people who form the natural background for all Balinese performances are missing.

In Bali, any place that is surrounded by a close-packed mass of humanity is a stage. The dances are designed to be seen from all sides, so that the background is always that of people. This background is so fascinating and so important that it is necessary to consider it as part of the performance. The KPM has also attempted to inject as much sex as possible into the dances, and sex is the one quality that is almost entirely absent from the Balinese dance, therefore its appearance strikes a false note. Furthermore, the KPM has, of necessity, employed the same dancers and orchestras over and over again because of the difficulty of bringing many people and instruments from great distances, and these particular musical clubs have received what, to them, is a considerable income.

They have been playing to an uncritical audience, which has little notion whether the performance is good or bad; consequently there has been a steady slackening of effort. These performances inevitably leave one with several misconceptions, and it is small wonder that many tourists return to their homes feeling bitterly disappointed with "paradise."

Because of the generalities indulged in by people publicizing round-the-world trips, and by others who are well-meaning but misinformed, many people have an impression that Bali is a land of "temple dancers," but this is far from being true. By "temple dancers" they usually mean legongs, who are most appealing because of their youth and grace, and consequently have been most often photographed. But legongs are in no sense temple dancers. Though they often perform at feasts and though Legong stories are based on old Hindu and Javanese legends, the Legong has little to do with religion—certainly far less than many other Balinese dances. The only true temple dancers in Bali are the old priests and priestesses who sometimes dance before an altar with offerings or flaming braziers. The performance of most dances or plays is not allowed in the temple, and only Redjang, Mendet, and Gabor are danced there regularly. The performance of Redjang is an offering in itself, while Mendet and Gabor are dances with offerings.

Late one night as I was passing through Penatih, I heard the tinkling melody of the gamelan and saw richly-clothed women passing into the temple with tall offerings on their heads. Inside, flickering oil lamps threw darting flames that pressed back the darkness. The temple was in the usual festive dress, and hundreds of people were coming and going, casting Gargantuan shadows on the walls. Girls followed their mothers, emulating their every movement; small boys grouped together and watched wide-eyed from a distance; dogs prowled about restlessly. The orchestra became silent shortly after I entered the temple, and some of the players sat back, chewing sirih or smoking, while others went to buy food or drink from the pretty dagangs who tended small tables just outside the temple. A pemangkoe, all in white, with a smoking brazier, went about the temple. Presently the gamelan struck up a melody and a woman in ceremonial dress commenced a slow dance. Her skirt, long and full in front, the point of greatest length being carried between the legs and extending in a train behind, swept the ground with each undulation of her body. She was joined by another woman and they danced a duet, crossing and recrossing the hard-packed earth of the temple courtyard; first slowly, then at an accelerated pace; dipping, bending, turning; the orchestra changing pace and complementing the rhythm of the dancers. White-clad pemangkoes made offerings all the while, moving from one shrine to another, trailing clouds of smoke perfumed with incense. When the two women tired, two more took their places, and after them, yet another couple, and another. This was Gabor. Hours later I left, but probably the people did not go home until dawn. Most of the children were still alert, though a few dozed in the laps of their brothers and sisters, and the babies slept in their mothers' arms. The scene was one of such simplicity and beauty, of such unquestioning faith and spiritual loveliness that it could be comprehended more easily emotionally than intellectually.

Mendet and Redjang are similar to Gabor. Both were danced with surpassing beauty at Asah, the costumes being remarkable for their beauty and their age, having been in the families of the girls for many generations. The headdresses and underskirts were the same in both dances. The headdresses were a profusion of pure gold flowers on a framework above a golden crown, the whole surmounted by a single tall spray of gold flowers springing directly from the back of the head. The crown, which just covered the hairline and framed the face, was set with semi-precious stones of different colors; and fresh flowers—jasmine, frangipani, and hibiscus—nestled amid the glittering gold. In the distended lobes of each girl's ears were huge soebangs, faced with gold and colored stones. The underskirts were either of solid colors, purple and blue, or of rich brocades in pastel shades on dark backgrounds, in designs of squares, hexagons, or circles.

For Mendet each girl wore a long strip of cloth, with gold leaf of floral or geometric pattern, wound about her torso, the two ends flowing down on either side. Tied over this was a sash of chrome yellow or robin's-egg blue. In her left hand she carried a silver or gold bowl, filled with yellow, red, and blue flowers, or covered with woven palm-leaf. From each tray hung a tracery of chartreuse palm-leaf cut into lovely, fragile designs. When these same girls danced Redjang they substituted for the gold appliquéd cloth which had originally been bound about their breasts, loosely woven overskirts of russet colors fastened above the breasts and hanging to within a foot of the ground.

For Mendet the girls gathered at the foot of the temple facing the mountains. They advanced ever so deliberately, as a single person, in three lines of five girls each, holding their colorful offerings in their left hands. Mendet is one of the slowest dances in Bali and appears to suggest motion rather than to move. One remembers the graceful hands, the upturned, slender fingers, the outstretched arms, the undulating movement, the undercurrent of the gamelan, and the almost mystic sense of consecration. The dancers finally came to the gate of the inner temple, and here the dance ended and they went inside to leave their offerings on the altar. Later they reappeared in their altered costumes to per-form Redjang. This time they formed four abreast and four deep. One end of the yellow, silken scarfs about the waist of each girl was held in the right hand of the girl directly in front of her, and the scarf of the girl first in line was thrown over her right shoulder. The outstretched arms of the dancers, slightly bent at the elbows, and the curved hands sug-gested the wings of birds in flight, and the gently flowing movement carried out the illu-sion. The yellow scarfs fell in graceful curves, giving continuity to each line, and throwing lovely complementary shadows on the earth. This dance, like Mendet, was ethereal, calm, and inspirational. With feet planted in earthly reality, the arms of the dancers, wing-like, lifted them toward the sublime heights of the gods.

Unlike Gabor, Redjang, or Mendet, which have no connection with drama, Legong is the danced interpretation of a story. There are several Legong stories which are taken from Hindu-Javanese sources, and all are danced by either two, or three, tiny girls be-tween the ages of six and twelve, to the accompaniment of a full pelegongan orchestra. Actually only the two principal dancers are called legongs, and they are dressed iden-tically; the third, their attendant, is called a tjondong, and is dressed more simply. The two small legongs of Sempidi wore skirts of purple cloth heavily appliquéd with gold, reaching from their waists to the ground. Their torsos were wrapped about with yards of narrow purple and green cloth, also appliquéd with gold. Attached to bodices of rough material were yellow sleeves studded with little mica mirrors. Their headdresses, jackets, belts, and a panel hanging in front to below their knees were all of elaborately filigreed buffalo hide, which was covered with gold leaf and set with little mirrors and precious stones. Their jackets were scarcely more than collars which stood out stiffly from their shoulders; from their belts, which behind became garoeda heads, hung loose streamers. Their headdresses were tremendously ornate, the base of each in the back also being formed by the head of a garoeda. This was surmounted by tiers of formalized leaves and the top was a mass of yellow frangipani flowers, while pink roses swayed gently on either side, like huge antennae.

Aside from the costumes, there are several stage properties which are a part of most Legong performances, such as wings, bows and arrows, and even Rangda masks. These properties appear in the dance, but no indication is given by shift of scene or costume that an actor or a dancer has suddenly changed from a butterfly into a nymph or from a beautiful heroine into a demon. Throughout the orient one imagines the background, which is either explained by a commentator or can be deduced from the stylized actions of the players. Thus a white cloth over the head of a Rangda denotes that she is invisible, while the same cloth in her hands, used in a certain manner, becomes a lethal weapon.

The sight of these small Legong dancers of Sempidi kneeling on a mat in front of the orchestra is one of my first recollections of the Balinese dance. I shall long remember this dance, which was given late one afternoon at a private feast, as it was my introduction to the Balinese audience. The small impassive faces of the dancers were covered with a light powder and their eyebrows were shaved and reshaped with a thick black makeup. Between their eyebrows was a white caste mark—now used purely as a decoration. There were several rows of children around the square which formed the dance floor. The youngest sat in front in little groups, their arms twined around one another, or supporting each other back to back. The smallest children were held in the laps of the older ones, or stood hugging their brothers and sisters, or laughed and played among themselves. A small girl sat on half a coconut husk with her knees drawn up and one hand held to her face. She remained in this position during most of the performance, conversing with the children who were facing her and paying little attention to the dancers. On the far side of the dance floor was a young girl with a small, naked baby, dressed in silver anklets, silver bracelets, and a large silver necklace. He stood tugging vigorously to get away while his sister held him. When he discovered that this was useless, he was not at all disturbed, but held her and touched his nose to hers, laughing all the while. The older children in the vicinity laughed back and appeared amused at his futile efforts. Little boys, not more than four or five years old, ran back and forth across the dance floor, getting lights for their cigarettes, which, however, contained no tobacco. Dogs wandered in and out, people called to one another across the square, the gamelan played a lilting melody, and the legongs danced on, their movements flowing, rhythmical, their faces set, as controlled as the movements of their arms and legs. Dogs or children were avoided skillfully without breaking the even rhythm and exquisite co-ordination between the two girls. They accelerated or slackened their pace as the music demanded. Their movements were angular, knees and elbows bent, backs arched, feet turned out, fingers curved to form slender crescents. Their fans became blurred segments of a circle. Their heads glided from side to side.

The dance twined in arabesques as complicated as the music, but the choreography of Legong is as circumscribed as that of classical ballet. Of its kind it is perfect, but it lacks the wide range of movement of many of the modern European and American dances.

I felt my eyes being drawn more and more to the audience who formed the colorful, magic square in which the legongs moved tirelessly. Here were a contented people who need not seek further for beauty. Behind the children were the women and the men. Children nestled in the laps of the gamelan players or slept among the instruments, even under the huge gongs. The dance wound on; a story of love, intrigue and battle. Here was all of Balinese life; the harmony of their society, the simplicity and beauty of their surroundings, their rhythmical and pictorial background, their gods, their kings, and the humble peasant. Here was beauty in dazzling gold and silk, and beauty in rags. Here was ugliness softened by a gracious manner. Here were discipline and freedom. Here was all of Bali wrapped up in sound and sight and smell.

I roused myself; I had been drugged by the music, or by my own thoughts. The Legong was over, and the crowd was leaving in little groups. The musicians were already carrying away their instruments. The small legongs sat on a piece of matting while someone wiped their damp faces. They were as imperturbable as ever.

On the road, lanterns and torches cast frantic shadows. People were laughing, small children stirring sleepily in their mothers' arms. Tomorrow night these same people would be part of another, yet the same, spectacle. These children would grow up to be dancers or musicians or priests. It is easy to understand why the Balinese ask nothing more than to be reincarnated in Bali in a future life.

Trance has a definite place in Balinese religious observance; mediums in trance consult with the spirits of the dead, and trance dancing—Sanghyang—is used as an antidote against sickness or misfortune in a village. Young girls, selected for their ability to fall easily into trance, are trained as sanghyangs when the occasion arises, and they may dance one night every week for months before their magic prevails over the evil force that is causing the trouble.

This was the case at Singapadoe. The young girls were prepared inside the temple. Supported from the rear by older women, they knelt before a smoking brazier while a pemangkoe recited prayers and fanned the smoke toward them. Outside the gamelan played. When the girls were considered to have entered sufficiently into a state of trance, they were dressed in traditional Legong costumes and carried by two men from the temple to a large shed. This shed was already crowded and was brightly lighted with gasoline storm lamps, which so often and so unbecomingly take the place of the native torches and oil lamps. The two little sanghyangs appeared dazed and stood dully until the gamelan struck up a melody. They then danced mechanically, without animation, floating on the music as in a dream phantasy, yet moving in perfect unison. Presently the orchestra was joined by a group of men in loin cloths, scarlet hibiscus flowers behind their ears. They formed into several compact concentric circles, the outer fringes of which were crowded by the audience. As the voices of the gamelan died, those of the men rose in a chant. A single voice soared above the others, silencing them, then all joined in again. This was the Ketjak circle. The chanting was rhythmical and powerful and was the prelude to motion. The bodies of the dancers, harshly lit by the storm lamp, pressed closer and closer together, motion grew from the center and imparted itself to the entire group. The bodies swayed rhythmically, then fell back on themselves and on the audience, while a priest recited a passage in Kawi. The swaying and chanting began again, then ended abruptly. For a while nothing happened; children in the audience scurried back and forth across the dance floor and the sanghyangs knelt on a mat as impassive as painted wooden figures. From the far side of the shed a group of women with white cloths wound about their breasts commenced a chant of their own, and when this was ended the gamelan took up once more, and the entire process was repeated several times before the meeting broke up.

From the Ketjak circle, which forms the vocal accompaniment to the Sanghyang, came the Ketjak, which tourists more often call the "monkey dance," because during the latter part of the dance the ketjaks are transformed into monkeys. The Ketjak group has been expanded to more than a hundred men and a story from the Ramayana has been added, though the exorcistic character of Sanghyang has remained, and the story is so unimportant that it is almost impossible to follow it in the dance. The Ketjak depends for its effect entirely on sound, rhythmic movement, and impact. There are only three generally-known Ketjaks in Bali, though it is impossible to say that there are not others— if one looks far enough one can usually find almost anything hidden away in a remote village where it is least suspected.

The beating of the koelkoel calls the dancers to the temple. From out of the darkness men appear in small groups, their kains girt up to form loin cloths. The figure of a high priest, his long hair flowing over his shoulders, is conspicuous among the sturdy peasants. In the center of a huge court is placed a standard, five feet high, on three sides of which descending nagas hold bowls in which lighted wicks are floated, while their upright tails support a large central bowl with three wicks. This is the only illumination for the dance. The men form about this hub in four concentric circles, leaving an open space in the center, perhaps twelve feet in diameter. Late-comers step over the others to gain the central circle or slip quietly into an inconspicuous place on the outer fringe. When all are in place, the talking and laughing suddenly cease. All bend their heads and stare intently at the ground. Suddenly, without warning, the surcharged atmosphere is rent by a shout issuing from a hundred throats. The figures are at once bolt upright, their hands above their heads, their extended fingers quivering. The shout dies into a hoarse whisper, a monotonous undertone which rises and swells. The upraised arms are crossed above the heads. The figures sway from side to side. On a downbeat all backs are suddenly bent, heads close to the ground, elbows resting on crossed legs, hands raised on either side of the bowed black heads, fingers still quivering. The pedanda steps into the center of the group and intones a story in a high-pitched, nasal voice. All at once the central circle rises and engulfs him, extended arms forming a pyramid above the flares. When they recede, the pedanda is still there. A lithe figure steals from out of the circling host and springs to sudden life inside the circle, opposite the pedanda. They harangue one another and dance slowly about the guttering flame, and then sink down and are lost in the multitude of fluttering hands and arms. Beyond the charmed circle of the dancers a crowd of men and women and small naked children have gradually collected. The chant rises and falls, the seated figures of the dancers sway forward and fall back, casting shadows like the opening petals of a huge lotus. They fall to the side and become four entwined chains of human bodies. An approaching shadow becomes the masked and winged figure of a garoeda, who dances briefly. The chant aspires toward a climax. Time and again excitement reaches heights that cannot be scaled. The pedanda enters the circle again, his long hair streaming wildly across his chest. His voice mounts in a frenzied wail, appealing to one side and then the other. Now the circle is broken and divided into two halves. The dancers, facing one another, have been transformed into hosts of monkeys and demons, both jabbering at each other, and stretching out their arms with widespread, fluttering fingers. One side rises in towering fury while the other sinks back, a prostrate mass, only to rise and overpower the other. Biting, screaming, clawing, the demons are finally triumphant, but the end is anti-climactic: when the battle is at its height, the dance suddenly ends, and the demons and monkeys walk off, arm in arm, into the night.

Another dance which borrows from the vocal accompaniment to the Sanghyang is the Djanger, but in its present form it bears no resemblance to its parent. Ten years ago almost every bandjar in Bali had its Djanger. It was the first really social dance that the Balinese ever had. The unmarried boys and girls of each community banded together to form clubs, and at each bandjar the dance developed differently. It borrowed freely from all sources and combined old forms with some new ones which were, to say the least, extraordinary. At Boeboenan there is supposed to have been a Djanger in which the girls wore one-piece bathing suits. This is really unthinkable; for a woman in Bali to expose her thighs is similar to a woman in this country appearing in public with her breasts uncovered. But the more extreme forms of the Djanger have already died out, and the dance itself is disappearing.

Today it is difficult to find a good Djanger, and probably the most colorful and best costumed one is that seen by the tourists at Kedaton. It is danced by twelve girls and twelve boys, six girls facing six others across a hollow square, with six boys on either of the other sides. Each girl wears a golden crown surmounted by three ascending rows of tightly rolled paper tubes radiating like rays of light in a semi-circle about her head. In some villages the Djanger crown is topped by white flowers. The girls' skirts are a vivid blue-green. Yellow cloths are wrapped tightly about their breasts and extend down around the hips. These in turn are covered from the breast to the waist by blue cloths with gold-leaf appliquéd. Around the neck of each dancer is an ornate circular collar of buffalo hide, delicately filigreed and covered with gold leaf. Their black hair hangs down in the back, and scarlet hibiscus flowers are set into it. The men wear kains of royal purple, mulberry-colored cloths bound about their torsos, and golden headcloths. Scarlet hibiscus flowers form brilliant dashes of color against the dark blue-black of their hair.

In addition to these players there is the Daag, the master of ceremonies, dressed in a long, flowing black coat with tight-fitting sleeves and a high waist. The Daag declaims the story as the girls sway gracefully to the strains of a small gamelan composed of drums and flutes, and the boys rock crazily from side to side, chanting unintelligible syllables. A girl dressed like the other girls, except that she wears a short, golden jacket and the elaborate headdress of a legong, dances a solo part. Toward the end of the dance these characters are joined by a garoeda, impersonated by an old man whose beard hangs down fantastically beneath the bird mask. He crouches and flutters his gilded wings and bobs his red and white tail feathers till vanquished by the soloist.

Anyone with a little imagination will soon find points of similarity between all Balinese dances, and it is really astonishing how great a variety of forms have been evolved out of a very slender repertoire of gesture. Thus Djoged and its variants, Gandroeng and Leko, are allied to Legong. The orchestra for Djoged is also similar to that employed for Legong, though bamboo instruments are substituted for iron ones, and fancifully carved figures holding flat pieces of bamboo over large jars take the place of the gongs. These gamelans are always gaudily painted and carved into curious figures.

After the djoged has performed the initial Legong sequence, the orchestra strikes up a different melody, and any man from the audience may now dance with her. The interest in the dance depends largely upon the ability of the man, and whether the djoged is skillful enough to follow his sometimes extremely complicated movements.

Gandroeng is identical to Djoged except that the girl soloist is supplanted by a young boy in the clothes of a legong; and Leko differs from Djoged only in that very young and unskilled dancers perform the solo parts.

At Bonah, Djoged was preceded by a performance of Leko. This dance had none of the abandon of Djoged. The man always kept very close to the small dancer, sweeping his outstretched arms about her and casting insinuating glances, but he was unable to coax the slightest sign of emotion from her. The entire dance seemed a caricature of passion.

The contrast between the small girl and the woman who followed in the Djoged was enormous. This woman danced in rapid succession with several partners, all of whom were accomplished dancers, each with a distinct style of his own. She was by far the most sensuous dancer that I ever saw in Bali. At first she danced rapidly with the man who had previously danced Leko with the younger girl. They advanced toward one another with bent knees and shuddered in the involved movement of the love dance. The dancer wooed the djoged, moving swiftly to the accelerated tones of the gamelan, and was quickly replaced by another man with two flaming hibiscus flowers in his batik headdress. He advanced toward the djoged with knees carried high toward his chest, arms flexed at the elbow, fingers quivering, passing her and turning back. In this movement she made no attempt to follow. He came close to her, caressing her with his eyes, one hand on his waist, the other hand barely touching her shoulder, suggesting an intimacy greater than was actually achieved. The lines of the arms and hands of the dancers formed graceful intertwining curves.

The drummer sprang up, twisting his kain into a loin cloth, advancing with arms held down as though to press the palms of his hands against the earth, his head tilted slightly back, his eyes turned up. He danced with abandon, passing close in front of the djoged and swinging his body backward to gaze another second into her face. They moved forward together, their arms crossed with geometric precision, and then separated to dance wide complementary circles and return again, he leaping into the air and advancing with most suggestive movements. A long-haired priest attempted to distract the djoged's attention from this dancer, and for a while the three danced together, both men wooing the djoged in turn, but the priest was finally unsuccessful and retired.

One of the most interesting performances in Bali is the Barong, which combines drama, dancing, mysticism, and frantic action in one exorcistic spectacle. Each performance of the play is preceded and followed by the making of offerings in the temple.

The play at Pagoetan starts with a slow dance by Barong, who dances delicately to the music, mincing forward, stopping suddenly as though perplexed, regarding the umbrellas quizzically, as though he has never seen them before and they are something strange and wonderful. He leans far forward, cocking his head to one side and gazing at them out of the corners of his eyes, and shakes his head dubiously. Then he reaches forward, gently sniffing them, and backs away, snapping his jaws and shaking his tail so as to make the bell at the end of it ring. This in turn interests him. He bends double in the center and regards it with curiosity, looking it up and down, turning away and then glancing back suddenly as though to surprise it. His open-mouthed wonder is astonishingly realistic, and his whole attitude is one of naive enjoyment of the most ordinary things.

Barong is followed by four girls wearing typical Djanger headdresses with fresh flowers trembling at the ends of the hollow tubes, red collars with silver beads, tight-fitting white bodices and fuchsia kains with narrow pink or yellow scarves bound about their breasts. They dance in pairs and are followed by a man in the costume of a legong who does a solo dance. The entrance of a patih, the prime minister of a prince, and his servant, announces the beginning of the drama.

The patih and his servant are passing through a haunted forest, and they are very much afraid. They glance nervously from left to right and speak fearfully. Finally they decide that it is not prudent to continue without first having the forest exorcized by a priest. The priest first haggles over the price he is to be paid and then brags that it is a very simple matter. Meanwhile a leyak, invisible because of the white cloth over its head, steals about, listening to all that is said and coming very close to the priest while he is bragging his loudest. The audience finds the duplicity of the priest and the antics of the leyak extremely amusing.

As soon as offerings have been made, the priest and his assistant depart, and at this moment the leyak becomes visible to the servant. His eyes bulge, but he appears incredulous and turns away, only to look back quickly. Meanwhile the leyak has become invisible and the servant is very much relieved, but just then the patih sees it as it is disappearing behind a group of children, who squirm about uneasily. Then it leaps over their heads amid laughter and cries. The patih and his servant are now thoroughly discomfited. While they are still uncertain whether or not to proceed, a strange procession passes through the forest; an old woman with sagging breasts leaning on a staff, two grave-diggers, and a man with two children. This man is wearing red and white striped trousers and a short cloth bound about his waist. His face and chest are covered with a yellow salve, and he carries one child whose face is covered with a white paste; the other child, who has white powder on his face and two yellow stars painted on his chest, walks beside him. At this point the plot is complicated by the appearance of a pregnant woman, played by a man, who is terribly scared by the leyak. She falls down upon the ground and gives birth to a male baby, who is promptly stolen by the leyak and its assistant, a small half-naked boy who darts about snatching things from the various players, who in turn are puzzled by the disappearances. Meanwhile, the man with the children sits huddled and trembling with fear until someone pours a bucket of water over his head. The audience rocks with laughter. This scene is largely extemporaneous and is never played twice in exactly the same manner.

Rangda comes out to stand on the steps of the temple, but she remains invisible. The play continues when the patih and his servant catch the leyak after a scuffle. When they discover what it is, they are frightened and don't know what to do with it. The prince enters and tells them to be calm; he will take care of everything. Rangda chooses this time to become visible, and the leyak is forgotten and escapes. The prince shouts a chal-lenge and rushes on Rangda with kris upraised and attempts to stab her. She falls back into the arms of an attendant, but immediately recovers and bests the prince in a fight. Barong joins the struggle, snapping his jaws and chasing Rangda away. But four more Rangdas appear, waving their arms above their heads, and the five hold unholy conference in a circle, their weird voices resounding fearfully. One of the Rangdas suddenly falls into trance and is carried into the temple, three disappear, and the highest manifestation of Rangda remains alone. Barong attacks Rangda again.

Meanwhile eight dancers, who have been prepared for their part in the temple, advance slowly in two lines of four each. They raise their knees high, stand for a long time and pivot on one foot. They are tense, and they grasp their krisses tightly. When Barong seeks their help, they rush at Rangda two at a time, uttering hoarse cries, their krisses raised. Their impact is terrific. Some fall before the glance of Rangda, others crash into her and she reels back, snapping her white cloth and uttering unintelligible sounds. The flying krisses rip into the thick hair that covers her, but she seems invulnerable and soon all the kris dancers are lying prostrate before her. Attendants place them on their backs in rows, their feet toward one another. Barong comes running to revive them and stands over each man, peering intently into his face and brushing it with his beard. A priest sprinkles holy water over the men. At first they come to life slowly, stirring uneasily and sitting up. They appear to be drained of all vitality, but suddenly they spring up and with great violence attempt to kris themselves. Two priestesses in trance appear with krisses, their long hair streaming wildly, the krisses pressed against their breasts. They throw themselves backward on one foot time after time, pressing down with all their strength on the krisses. Several men attempt to stop them, but they cannot; the strength of trance is too great.

A pemangkoe dressed in white goes among the dancers with a smoking censer, holding it beneath the drooping faces of the entranced men. Some of them become passive and the krisses are taken from them, but others reel away and start once more to kris themselves, uttering moans or wild shouts, and as many as five or six men are required to wrest a kris from a dancer's hands. One dancer dashes the burning coals into his face and tries to bury his face in the censer. But in the end he is restrained and collapses suddenly. The last dancers are overcome and the priestesses are carried, still struggling, into the temple.

Here the play ends with the triumph of good over evil. The power of Barong has restored the villagers to life and has prevented the krisses, turned against them by Rangda, from piercing their bodies. But the Balinese are fearful of displeasing the evil spirits, so the play never reaches its logical conclusion, the destruction of Rangda. She merely disappears, and one is allowed to imagine the rest.

The orchestra and the audience have already started home, but within the temple the drama is still unfolding. The scene is one of confusion. Four kris dancers and the two priestesses are stretched out before an altar on which rest several Rangda masks, their long gold and red tongues hanging down. Barong wanders aimlessly about the court, coming up to the altar, gazing at the offerings and snapping his jaws. He is alive! He is still Barong! He has conquered! He has brought the villagers back to life! He glowers at the Rangda masks, resting his weight uneasily first on one foot, then on another and swaying unsteadily; the leading player has fallen under the spell of his role. He is supported, as the body of Barong is lifted from him, and then falls forward, foam flecking his lips, and is laid with the others.

A pemangkoe sits in prayer facing offerings set out on a woven palm-leaf mat in front of the altar. He is assisted by two old women dressed in white with white cloths bound loosely over their breasts.

Darkness is settling over the temple, and the flickering lights of oil lamps make the scene even more ghostly. The women are still in deep trance and have not stirred. The smoke eddies in ascending spirals; a few villagers hover in the background; the Rangda masks, half covered by their sacred white cloths, still rest with tongues extended, like the heads of disembodied spirits. The actor who has played the part of Barong moans, and efforts are made to revive him. His mouth works spasmodically but his eyes are closed and his spirit seems to be groping toward something. He feels that part of the ceremony has not been completed. The men who have been supporting him lift him to a sitting position, and he gains partial control of his body, though his spirit seems to linger in another world. The pemangkoe produces a baby chick from a covered basket. Holding it in the palms of his hands so that its head extends from between his thumbs and forefingers, he passes it rapidly through the incense-smoke of a brazier. The actor eagerly takes the chick from the pemangkoe and holds it in his hands. His eyes are burning as he extends the chick toward the altar and moves his hands back and forth through the smoke. Suddenly he thrusts its head into his mouth and chews violently, but his strength is inadequate and the body dangles, writhing, from his jaws. Another man tries to stop him, but he clamps his jaws the more firmly and the other pulls the body of the chick from the head. The actor chews vigorously and swallows. Then, the necessary ceremonies having been performed and the spirits appeased, he rouses a bit and takes some arak. The spirit of Barong has left him now, and he seems normal, though weak. Somewhere within the courtyard a man laughs, and the spell is broken.

The air seems fresher outside the temple. Though it is dusk, men and women are still bathing in the river. The murmur of their voices and soft laughter rise from the chasm through which the river flows.

Music weaves a protective pattern over the island. It is a part of all feasts and ceremonies. It sets the key for every occasion. To the Balinese it is as necessary as breathing.

We are on our way to Bonah to hear the Kebyar Gong, considered to be one of the finest in Bali. The night air is caressing and the young moon casts a luminous pathway, patterned with the black threads of newly planted rice. The terraces are dark walls devoid of detail, projected on the shimmering water. Pin points of light, which might be either leyaks or the torches of villagers, move along the narrow paths between the sawahs. At Soekawati the road overflows with people who are watching a shadow play, and at Blah-batoeh the gamelan is practicing, as it has every night for the past month. Fragments of sound drift on the air. The players are working out a new piece. In a few weeks it will be finished. At Blega an Ardja—Balinese operetta—has just begun. It is being held in a large roofed enclosure, at one end of which curtains are drawn and from behind them issues a plaintive voice preparing the audience for the appearance of the character to which it belongs. Presently the curtains part, and we learn that this is the servant of a princess. She comes forward slowly, her hands fingering the curtain which she holds about her. After a long while, she begins a circling dance, all the time singing and entreating her mistress to come forth. Ten minutes pass and the drama has progressed no further. The sweet voice of the princess can be heard from within the small enclosure made by the curtains, and occasionally a shadow drifts along the wall, but her servant still winds about the stage, describing her mistress's charms and telling her that all has been prepared. Ardja is endless, so we leave, planning to stop on our return.

At Bonah the sound of the gamelan comes from the end of a long lane, and the lovely, intricate undercurrent of the gangsas draws us closer. The musicians sit in a hollow square, illumined by the soft light of oil flares. All about are the villagers, close-packed, and behind them an intimation of temple walls and huge gates. Already the night is permeated with the singing overtones, the delicate counterpoint, the rhythm, the penetrating melody, the bubbling effervescence of the gongs; an ecstatic overpowering flood of music, a con-fusion of sound multiplied and compounded, out of which rise the thin notes of the melody, clear bell-like chimes limned against the deep undertone.

The drums give depth, perception, and a tremendously exciting quality to the music. The fingers of the drummers fly faster and faster, the whole gamelan melts into incredible intricacies of polyphony. The clear notes of melody spring out, unmistakable, transparent, and lovely. Again the counterpoint rolls over the melody, the pace slackens, and a new voice enters, making its way calmly through the background of sound. It drifts on a clear sea of sound and is mirrored in its depths. It is taken up and elaborated, while the mind is captivated, enchanted, drugged, the senses glutted with the intricacy of the tonal back-ground. Suddenly the gamelan is silent. There has been no crashing climax. The melody has simply run itself out.

The drummers shift their positions, the trompong player strolls off; the drums take up again, and the gangsas ring out clearly. Two dancers stand in the shadows, one on either side of the large gongs. On a sudden downbeat both enter and move swiftly; interpreting the music. This is not Legong, though many of the gestures of Legong are used; it is pure musical interpretation. The dancers move with lightning swiftness, with incredible precision, with a lovely, flowing movement growing out of the torso, their knees bent, their feet turned up, the incredible syncopation of the gamelan urging them on. Now they are on their knees, their fans fluttering, their bodies curving to the ground on either side, weaving a phantasy of motion amid the complex sound. This is a sight to be seen a hundred times, music to be heard a thousand times. It must enter into one's blood; possess one gradually.

Women with babies in their arms stand in the shadowy background. Grandfathers with their small grandsons between their knees sit close to the gamelan. The dancers move tirelessly. People come to listen for a time and then move on. The girls with their little food stands ring the audience, and boys sit behind them, flirting and talking. At one a child not more than three years old is waiting to be served, and the inevitable dogs mope about. When do these people sleep? Is there never an end to dancing and music? Is there nothing to mar this Paradise? Perhaps—but the people have exorcized it with beauty. This is the life of the village; there is no other; but there is enough of this enchanted music, of these dances, these characters, and these legends for a lifetime—for many lifetimes. The marvel increases with familiarity. Each note, each motion, each costume, conveys something new. It is a part of an ancient tradition; it is deeply felt.

Long after midnight we returned to Blega. Comic characters were romping about the stage and the audience was rocking with laughter at their antics. Though it was late, the drama had little more than started. We were already saturated with the tumultuous music of the Kebyar Gong. To the people all this was as ordinary as the planting of a field or the eating of rice, but the lovely melodies of the gamelan still haunted us. The rhythmic interpretation of the dancers, their absolute precision, their tirelessness, all filled our thoughts. There was no room for Ardja or for anything else.

To most people the Kebyar will conjure up the image of a dancer seated cross-legged, with his long kain flowing to one side, the upper part of his body encased in a cloth of blue and gold, his head bound about with a golden headdress, and behind his ear a scarlet hibiscus; his marvelously mobile face and flying fingers interpreting the music, his body bent as though by the force of a hurricane. They will remember the strange motion of the crossed legs which propelled him about the stage, the way he hovered gracefully by one of the instruments, his fan fluttering like the wings of a humming-bird. They will see him playing the trompong with a lightness of touch and a remarkable clarity of tone, dancing as he plays, with half-closed eyes, swaying, twirling the sticks, and suddenly leaving the instrument to whirl again about the floor.

This is Mario. It was he who composed this particular interpretation of the Kebyar music, and there has never been anyone to equal him. Though he has been sick and seldom dances any more, neither the incredible precision of Goesti Raka nor the sensuous interpretation of Rindi can match him. He still teaches at Tabanan, and it is fascinating to watch him propel his young pupils about the floor, pushing up their chins, stretching out their arms, and molding their fingers. Sometimes he dances in front of them, but usually behind, lifting them from their feet, whirling them about the stage, and laughing when they fall; his every gesture so expressive that words would be superfluous. In the background a huge banyan tree forms a natural amphitheater and during the lesson many children climb high into it and peer out from between the leaves like elves in a fairy tale.

One night at Bebetin in North Bali we came upon a Kebyar Gong practicing in a roofed enclosure by the road. The North Bali gamelan is characterized by the demoniac manner in which the players attack their instruments. It seems impossible that anything can result except the greatest amount of noise, yet so precise are the players that the effect is often spectacular, and, under a tin roof, deafening. We sat among the villagers while the gamelan played on, stopping occasionally to revise a passage. The deep tones of the gongs struck through our bodies. The syncopated rhythm coursed through our veins like blood.

Two girls appeared quite suddenly and began to dance. They were in everyday dress with only a kain about their waists, and the effect was very different from that produced by the tightly bound torsos of the dancers in an actual performance. It heightened the effect produced by the abandon of the music.

This spectacle of sound and sight outstripped the senses. The voices of the gamelan were entwined in an ever-increasing complication. Rhythm and counter-rhythm opposed each other, and syncopation ruled supreme. Then the music stopped, the dancers walked calmly away; the terrific tension of the drummers dropped from them. They stretched casually as though they had but recently risen from a nap.

Baris is seen in many varied forms throughout the island. One hears that there are more than forty different types of ceremonial Baris alone, and it is easy to believe this.

High Priest 49

50   *Orchestra at Paksebali*

Mendei at Asah 51

52   *Actor in Wajang Wong*

Dancing Barong 53

54   Cremation at Tabanan

Koelkoel Koekoelan

Cremation Tower

Temple Feast

Priest Dancing

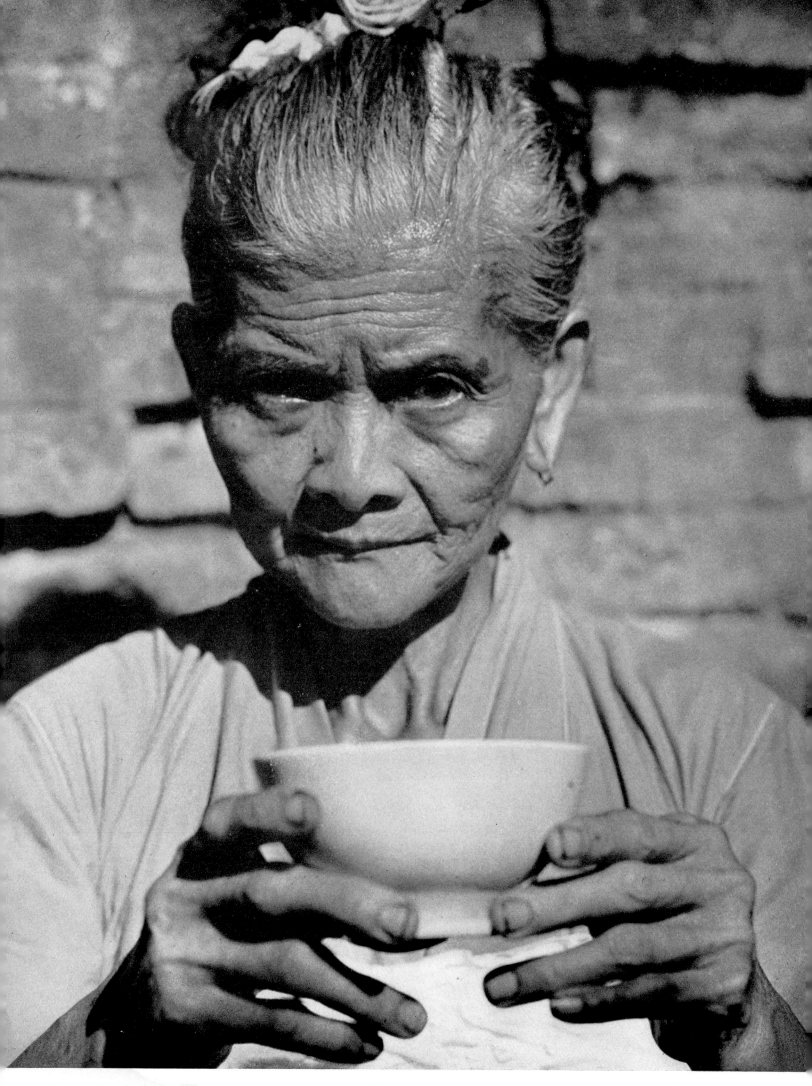

Priestess 59

60   *Large Lamaks at Oeboed*

Elaborate Offerings 61

62   *Low Caste Priest*

Baby Dressed for Temple Feast

Redjang at Asah

The various ceremonial Barises of the mountain villages can be distinguished largely by the weapon that is carried. Many of these dances are performed in a slovenly fashion which is unlike the Balinese, but with ceremonial Baris the fact of the performance satisfies religious demands, and the manner in which it is performed is unimportant. This was certainly so at Kedisan on Lake Batoer, where we witnessed Baris Toembak and Baris Dap-dap. The former was performed with long red spears. The dancers wore triangular headdress with small tapered pieces of painted wood set on springs, narrow white trousers and close-fitting shirts, many-colored stoles and wide pieces of red, green and black cloth with gold appliquéd, and about their necks wide collars covered with colored beads. Each dancer also wore a kris with a golden handle, and a hibiscus flower behind his ear. These same costumes were worn later for Baris Dap-dap, though shields of heavy buffalo hide a foot in diameter, painted and gilded to look like huge flowers, were substituted for the spears. The eight dancers seemed never to have rehearsed together before and only one or two had any idea of what form the dance should take. The most characteristic step of Baris Toembak was a hesitation on one leg while the knee of the other leg was drawn far up, the foot bent at an angle, and the heel pointed toward the knee. The dancers advanced in two lines with the butts of the spears held in their hands, the spears towering above them. This was followed by a slow movement in a crouching position with the butts of the spears held toward the central shrine of the temple. There was little more to this Baris than the slow advance, occasionally shifting the spears, or laying them on the ground and dancing around them.

In Baris Dap-dap, as with Baris Toembak, the dance was begun at the end of the temple, away from the shrine. The first four dancers held shields, the last four conventionalized bows and arrows. There was the same slow advance with the typical high step, the knee almost touching the chest of the dancer; but in the latter part of the dance, the men split into groups of four, those in each group forming a square and facing toward its center. Here the ingenuity of the leaders ran out, and there was some discussion as to what should follow, but no decision could be reached and the dance broke up.

At Djoelah in North Bali there is an entirely different type of Baris performed by children with offerings. Unlike the dancers at Kedisan, these children are beautifully trained and dance with the utmost assurance. Two boys are dressed in the true Baris costume, even to the krisses, and two small girls wear Legong headdresses and long dresses touching the ground, with sashes tied about their waists, and brocaded collars and aprons. The two boys danced first, holding silver bowls with offerings. Long streamers of palm-leaf flowed from the bowls, which also held colorful flowers. The boys danced in simple patterns toward a shrine, finally laying their offerings down and continuing to weave about one another, making long sweeping curves with their arms, the palms of their hands turned out and the arms slightly bent at the elbow. The two girls then danced in a similar fashion, though without offerings, and then all four danced together. The youngest child could not have been more than five, and the oldest was certainly no more than eight. This dance was quite dissimilar to every other Baris that I have seen.

Dramatic Baris has evolved from the simpler Baris forms, and in its final state it has become a series of solo dances, usually bound together by a story from the Ramayana. Many of these dances are incredibly splendid in their appearance and their movements, and each dancer gives a highly individualized performance. Some stories call for as many as six or eight dancers, and no village has that many Baris dancers of real distinction. Consequently it is seldom that one sees a first-rate performance, for when dancers must come from distant villages, there are a thousand reasons why they do not arrive.

Dramatic Baris is very different from ceremonial Baris. It is one of the most characteristic of Balinese dances. The dancer, heroic in his glittering, vibrant headdress and his many-colored stoles, emerges from between ceremonial umbrellas much as does Barong, and he treats the umbrellas in a very similar fashion. He gazes at them with rapt attention, or with disbelief. His movements are rapid and have tremendous vitality. Here is no common hero, no polished prince, but either a god or a demon, who moves rapidly about the stage or draws himself to his full height, his eyes bulging, his expression disdainful. His body is supported by one leg, the other bent at the knee and raised from the ground, and one hand grasps his stoles and holds them below his chin.

There are several Baris stories; all from the Ramayana and each ending in a combat. Every Baris dancer, at his first appearance, performs a stylized dance which has nothing to do with the story but is the dancer's introduction. This is a very common thing in the Balinese theater and so conventional is the approach that the dancers or actors themselves very often do not know until long after the play has started which story they are acting.

The characters of Dramatic Baris are like those in other Balinese performances. Each Baris dancer has his comic servant who imitates him and satirizes his every movement, often so cleverly that he steals the show. The clown is always the favorite of the Balinese audience because his jokes are understandable and his ambitions and fears similar to its own. There is also the heroine and her servant, and often one or more leyaks or rangdas.

The scenes in which rangdas are left on the stage with the servants of the Baris dancers are screamingly funny to the audience and are a mad roughhouse. The servants often climb up the sides of buildings, hide behind the audience or ceremonial umbrellas, or run away, only to return. Rangda may appear suddenly behind the back of one of the servants, who naturally is unaware of her presence. But the other servant suddenly looks up and is transfixed by the apparition hovering over his friend. So frightened is he that he cannot speak but makes wild motions with his hands which puzzles the other, who imitates his movements, not knowing what he means. Finally Rangda utters a ferocious growl, and the servant turns around to find her looking into his face. As likely as not he dives through Rangda's legs and scrambles off on all fours. Rangda then pursues the second man, but the first rapidly recovers and kicks Rangda soundly from behind. This hilarious slapstick is kept up until the sudden appearance of a Baris dancer, who advances to give battle. The servants then become very brave, but the moment Rangda turns upon them they flee to the protection of the Baris dancer.

Another favorite scene is that of two Baris dancers sitting in meditation on either side of the dance ground. The heroine enters and performs a dance of temptation before them, but they are oblivious to her, though the servants attempt to attract the attention of their masters. The heroine dances seductively around each of the dancers, but it is a long time before either displays any sign of recognition. Finally the meditation of one is disturbed, and he rises to dance with the heroine. The servant of the second dancer then becomes frantic and finally rouses his master who rises in a fury and drives off the first dancer and himself dances a highly erotic love dance with the heroine. This precipitates a fight between the two dancers in which the servants take part, each urging on his master.

The fierce restless movement of the Baris dancer is here brought to its highest perfection. Each dancer becomes possessed of fearful energy and seems superhuman in his dynamic, quivering, scintillating splendor. The combat is slowly joined, each dancer at first attacking only when the other's back is turned and rushing off when his opponent turns to face him. Finally, with drawn krisses, the dancers rush at each other and clash in a frenzied combat of whirling stoles, jumping high into the air, and landing with knees fully bent, in a combat strangely reminiscent of the ruffling feathers and brilliant leaping and whirling of fighting cocks. One of the dancers is finally driven off, but he may return in the form of Rangda, a higher power, to avenge himself. The Baris dancer, who himself appears to be a character of demoniac power, here triumphs over Rangda or another Baris dancer, who represents an evil force. It appears to be a question of one demon triumphing over the other, or of the gods possessing to some extent the characteristics of demons.

It is difficult to interpret the character of the Baris dancer, and one is reminded that the Balinese make no clear distinction between gods and demons. It is as important to them to propitiate one as the other, and one wonders whether they do not consider good and evil as different manifestations of the same force.

In addition to the ordinary theater, there are two very interesting dances connected with the rice harvest; one, Koelkoel Koekoelan, the other Djoged Boem Boem. Koelkoel Koekoelan is performed in several villages near Marga north of Tabanan. In it a man dances on a huge drum which is pulled through the rice-fields. In his hand he holds a large hammer, its head shaped like a watermelon, and he periodically punctuates his dance by beating on the drum. He is accompanied all the while by an orchestra of ten men in groups of five, beating on two long bamboo poles and producing a staccato rhythm. This dance is very restricted in movement. Djoged Boem Boem is performed at Tabanan by five women in long blue kains with a design of green and yellow and orange woven into them. Their breasts are tightly bound in cloth with an appliquéd design of gold, which is partially covered by a sash of yellow and orange, and their black hair is coiled on the back of their heads and covered with sprays of yellow, orange, and red flowers. The accompaniment is played by five men, who drop bamboo rods onto a long narrow table. Each bamboo varies in length from two to three feet, and each produces a different sound. The rods are bounced with one hand and caught with the other, precisely as the women use them when pounding rice. These hollow bamboos produce a very interesting rhythmic background for the dancers, who wind about with fluttering fans and mobile fingers, at times stretching out their arms gracefully, like the slow wheeling of birds in flight.

This world of movement, of melodic, syncopated sound, of color, of glittering ornament, and of religious mysticism is the ever-present background of Balinese life. To us who go to a play or to a musical recital to be entertained or to gratify a passing desire, it will seem astonishing that these ornaments of our life are as important to the Balinese as eating and sleeping and working. Theirs is a well-balanced and a full life because each day brings both the sweat and the delight of living.

6

Its very impermanence has preserved Balinese architecture as a living art.

ALMOST every country where civilization has existed for more than a few hundred years has its architectural remains; its Pyramids, its Stonehenge, or its Taj Mahal; dead tombs which are carefully preserved and which the tourist is usually shown in preference to living monuments. In countries where nothing is left but the fragments of a glorious past, this may be justified: there is certainly nothing in present-day Javanese civilization to compare to the Boroboedoer or to the temples of Prambanan, nor in Cambodia anything that approaches the magnificence of Ankor Wat or Ankor Thom; and it is refreshing, therefore, to find in Bali an architecture firmly rooted in the past yet being constantly renewed and augmented—one which is alive.

Contemporary Balinese architecture is almost entirely confined to temples, for the once-splendid palaces of the princes have either fallen into disrepair or have given way to ugly cement buildings, pseudo-European in character; and the homes of even the wealthiest villagers are built of mud and thatch to a common pattern. The most elaborate have only a few carved beams, or a thicker thatch to distinguish them from the poorest.

At Mabi in North Bali and at Poepoean in South Bali I have seen quaint figures of animals, particularly dogs, made of black palm fiber, which stood on the ridges of houses. There are also occasional, elaborate rice barns, tall structures with half-oval roofs of thatch two feet thick, set upon seemingly inadequate pillars with flared capitals designed to keep out the rats. I saw one such rice barn at Tegaltamoe. It had a carved doorway at one of the gabled ends, the sill of which was at least ten feet from the ground. The outer edge of the gable was supported by two pillars which rested on the backs of winged dragons, and the doorway was set back perhaps three feet into the gable. The door itself was painted green and gold, whereas the columns, the dragons and other ornaments were blue and yellow. The whole had the effect of a shrine, and this may have been the intention.

The Balinese temple is no huge building where people worship, shut away from sunlight and starlight. It may have one, two, three, or even more courtyards, in which there are varying numbers of balés and shrines. A temple may be with or without meroes—the many-roofed pagodas so common to the Balinese landscape; it may have ornate koelkoel towers, or the koelkoels—hollow logs which are beaten to call the villagers together—may be hung in trees; there may be balés for pilgrims, for orchestras, for offerings, or there may be nothing but a few small shrines; there may be god-seats and pavilions, sculptured figures or none, walls with or without bas-reliefs, or no walls at all. Whenever possible there are frangipani trees whose gnarled trunks and long dark-green, crescent-shaped leaves and delicately perfumed yellow flowers soon become associated with all the temples of Bali.

One of the most striking features of Balinese temple architecture is the huge gateways that lead into most temples, and from one courtyard to another. They are of two types, the split gateway—tjandi bentar, and the covered ceremonial gateway—padoe raksa. The tjandi bentar is generally the gateway to the outer temple and the padoe raksa to the inner, but their positions may be reversed, or two gates of either type may be used. The ceremonial gateway, as the name implies, is, in many temples, used only on particular occasions, and a small gateway in the inner wall is used at all other times.

The size of a temple is no indication of its holiness; size and profuse decoration are rather an index to the wealth of a community and to the number of its builders, sculptors and carvers. One of the guardian temples of the island is a tiny shrine.

Subjects for sculpture and decoration are never lacking in Bali. There are designs such as the swastika and Greek fret which are to be found in all countries of the world; there are formalized leaf and flower patterns; there are masks and the Bhoma face used above most ceremonial gateways; there are sculptures of princes, rangdas, and raksasas—demons; there are scenes from literature and drama, and in North Bali, scenes of seduction and beer drinking, in which white men appear. There is also a certain amount of pornographic material. All things appear to be material for the Balinese artist. The figures, however, are never worshipped. A Balinese temple is meant to be a pleasant resting place for the gods during their stay on the island, and most shrines are empty except for offerings of food and flowers.

Bali is a land of unnumbered temples—perhaps forty thousand is too low an estimate

—and as the only material available is a soft sandstone called paras and an equally soft native brick, all of them must be constantly renewed or repaired, with the exception of a few primitive Bali Aga temples in the mountains built of stones piled roughly one on the other, and several temples on the beach built of loose coral. The beautiful temple at Serangan made of perfectly fitted and finely carved blocks of coral is unique. This temple is notable for its simplicity, and the Balinese, with the primitive tools at their disposal, would have great difficulty in duplicating their usual rococo ornamentation in such a hard material. The use of paras, therefore, has rendered Balinese architecture so impermanent as to insure its vitality, and it has made possible the lacy tours de force of North Bali.

The damp, hot climate also plays its part in the destruction of Balinese temples. Six months after a temple has been completed, a soft patina of red and grey lichen gives it an ageless air, and in a year the tropical vegetation has commenced to disintegrate the intricate carvings of a gateway, and ferns may be growing from a thatched roof. For this reason archeological remains are all but non-existent. The Kings' Tombs near Tampaksiring and some figures in the temple atop the mountain at Panoelisan, and a few more at Tjatoer, are rare examples of eleventh century Hindu art.

At Tista, a remote town in East Bali, there is a primitive altar in the temple, set with the broken fragments of flat stones. At the rear of this altar, which is perfectly square, there are several thin, triangular stones placed in a semi-circle about a very old stone carving, apparently a phallus, though highly conventionalized. The Balinese preserve these remnants of a forgotten age because of their reverence for the spirits of their ancestors, but they do not worship them any more than they do the contemporary sculptures which decorate all of their temples.

The master-builder in Bali has never become an architect, and the Balinese artist remains an artisan. The splendid temple gateways are in the minds of the builders, and plans are seldom drawn. The construction of a temple, like all things in Bali, is conducted in a seemingly haphazard fashion, yet it is eventually completed in a way quite satisfactory to the community.

The need for a temple may be announced by a priest or an inspired medium, who may also announce the new location. The old temple may or may not be abandoned when a new one is built. In either case, work is allotted by the village council, and if there are no skilled craftsmen in the community, which happens only occasionally, they will be hired from other villages. Work on the temples is considered to be as much a part of the individual's responsibility to his community as agriculture, and payment is made only to outsiders. A general plan is discussed; after that, builders, sculptors, and carvers spend as much time as they can spare from the fields, and work may progress quickly or slowly, depending upon the season and the number of craftsmen available.

Paras is cut from the soft cliffs by the rivers in blocks of approximately the sizes to be used in the temple. Sometimes huge pieces of sculpture are carved from a single block and as many as twenty men will struggle to drag it from a ravine to the temple. In South Bali the putty-colored paras is usually combined with a dark red brick and the two become quickly blended, the paras turning almost black and the brick becoming softened by green and yellow lichen. Both brick and paras are laid without mortar and are fitted perfectly by rubbing adjoining blocks together until the joints are smooth. The parts to be decorated are put up in the rough and are later sculptured while in place, but, due to Balinese laissez-faire, many temples are never finished and parts of others are already collapsing before the last bit of carving has been completed. This is less astonishing, however, than that such massive and incredibly rococo temples as those of Koeboetambahan and Sangsit in North Bali have been conceived and built by peasants in their leisure time.

One of the most magnificent temples in Bali is the great complex at Besakih. It is high up on the shoulder of the Goenoeng Agoeng and dominates the surrounding countryside. Its dramatic background is the steep slope of the mountain. Originally the temple was far from the nearest village, but a little community has recently grown up about its base, and today a series of smaller temples lead up to the foot of the great seven-tiered wall guarded by forty raksasas and dominated by a huge split gateway. From a distance, the ornate ceremonial gateway to the inner court towers even higher.

Besakih, in spite of its size, is simple. The first court contains a number of balés set about a central square which is dominated by three tall god-seats. The huge inner court rises in a series of uneven brick steps to an upper court with a few small shrines and a number of five-, seven-, nine-, and eleven-storied meroes; but all about the temple proper are more meroes, rising in graceful tiers against the cloudy sky. From the topmost terrace, a glorious panorama of black palm-fiber roofs, of beige brick-work, of chrome yellow fields, and sunlit foliage extends to the hazy coastline.

Almost any tourist who has stayed in Bali for as much as a week has seen Besakih. He has been told that it is the most sacred temple of the entire island, and he has been charged twenty-five cents for the privilege of admission. But Besakih is the temple of the radjas who come every year to the great temple feast to make offerings and to pray. To the ordinary peasant Besakih seems austere and distant. It is on the same plane, in his mind, as the mighty Hindu gods whom he has revered from afar, but who are too high and too mighty to be concerned with the small problems of his everyday life. Besakih is unquestionably very holy, but its greatest influence is in its own neighborhood, and there are other great temples which dominate the more distant sections of the island.

Another temple which the tourist is almost bound to see is the one built around the Sacred Springs at Tampaksiring. It is an unimposing temple, but the springs are reputed to have great healing powers, and people from all about come to bathe there. In the inner courtyard the springs bubble up into a pool of crystal-clear water, and two long pools separated by a high wall, one for men and the other for women, are fed from the overflow, the water pouring in from a dozen naga heads.

Tampaksiring has unfortunately been largely appropriated by Europeans, who have built a rest house on the hillside above the temple—desecration in itself—and a large swimming pool just outside the temple gateway.

The Kings' Tombs near Tampaksiring have also been commercialized. These tombs are in a narrow gorge of the Pakrisan River which is fed by the Sacred Springs. There are nine monumental tombstones carved in high relief into the limestone cliffs. Each tomb has its own oval niche, and there are four on one side of the river and five on the other side, facing each other. These tombs date from the eleventh century, and one of them is supposed to be the resting place of the brother of the famous Balinese king, Erlangga, whom he left to rule Bali while he himself ruled East Java. Next to the tombs there is a rock monastery carved from the cliff on the eastern side of the river. It is not unusual, even today, to find a few small offerings at the base of the tombs, testifying to the Balinese's reverence for their deified ancestors. The tombs, however, remain something of an enigma, and it has never been adequately proved either that they were tombs or that the stone cells were in reality a monastery.

The great temple complex on the slopes of Goenoeng Batoekaoeh, the second highest mountain on the island, is fully as sacred as that of Besakih, though it has a more intimate setting. The temple is reached by a jungle trail and is entirely surrounded by a wall of green trees and tangled lianas. As at Besakih, there are several subsidiary temples, but those of Batoekaoeh are tiny buildings little higher than a man, with thatched roofs and walls of woven bamboo matting. They are set in the midst of over-arching trees which in turn are surrounded by clean-swept clearings in the jungle. There is also a sacred spring, guarded by raksasas; but the most unusual thing about this temple is the illusion that everything is green. Not until later does one realize that the effect is produced by the grass which covers both the inner and outer temple courtyards. This is very unusual in Bali, where the floors of most temples are of hard-packed earth, which becomes a deep brown after a rain, and at other times, rises in a powdery, light dust.

There is no imposing entrance to the temple at Batoekaoeh; only an exceptionally wide and low split gateway, entirely covered by soft green moss and overshadowed by a huge tree. The outer court is a huge rectangle with a balé for the orchestra, a cooking shed, and two huge balés running parallel to its length. The buildings of the inner courtyard, as at Besakih, are almost all meroes, but the effect at Batoekaoeh is very different, for none of the meroes have more than seven roofs, and most have three or five. They are all raised on low stone platforms and are built of a lustrous weathered wood and set about with small green and red shrubs. In the entire temple there are only a few conservative figures of guardian raksasas, and there is unusual restraint in ornamentation. The whole effect is one of delicately modulated tones, of agelessness and serenity.

No temple in Bali could form a greater contrast to the garish splendor of the almost overwhelming architecture of North Bali than that of Batoekaoeh. A small section of the country in the neighborhood of Sangsit, Koeboetambahan, and Menjali is the source of most of this fantastic innovation. There are, of course, many elaborate temples in South Bali, but the most fanciful of them pales before the demon faces which spring from every gateway, the tenuous ornamentation, and the brilliant color with which the stone in North Bali temples may be outlined and accentuated.

The conception of architecture in North Bali is, in any case, quite different from that of South Bali, though the essential form of the temple remains. The North Bali gateways tend to be more massive, the ceremonial gateways often having three doorways, and the shrines become more and more concentrated in a few highly ornate buildings. This is particularly true of one temple in a bandjar of Sangsit, where the ceremonial gateway is fully twenty-five feet high and thirty feet wide at its base. It is pyramidal in shape, and the nine wide stone steps leading to the central doorway complement the serrated top. The entire face of the gateway is covered by the heads of demons and dense masses of sculptured leaves. The demon heads, with their long, curving white tusks, stand out in very high relief, and at noon throw deep shadows which give them the appearance of hovering above the doorway. Within the second courtyard is a tremendous L-shaped structure culminating at the center of one side of the L in a huge shrine with a tiled roof with nagas on the ridge, raising their heads above the eaves. There is a stone stairway leading directly to this shrine and another stairway at a corresponding place in the other arm of the L. Many of the shrines, which in South Bali require a dozen buildings, here are united. The entire mass is covered with pinnacles of intricately carved stone rising from each terrace. The figures of demons on the terrace walls are in the same deep relief as those on the ceremonial gateway. If one looks long enough at this fantastic stone foliage, one has the feeling that demon faces peer at one, even out of the conventionalized leaf forms.

This temple has some fine old frangipani trees whose gnarled trunks rise in convolutions as weird as the architecture. The design of the entire temple is full of the same restless energy which pervades North Balinese music. There is only one jarring note: one of the balés is roofed with corrugated iron. Unfortunately, this is not peculiar to this particular temple. It is the curse of North Bali, where there are whole towns with scarcely a thatched roof to be seen anywhere. One tale, probably apocryphal, has it that an over-zealous official condemned all grass and palm-thatched roofs because of the danger of conflagrations from the backfires of passing automobiles. The storyteller invariably adds, with a touch of malice, that this is a tribute to the business-like Dutch. Whatever the origin of the corrugated iron, its existence is to be regretted, for it is hideous as well as expensive. It is also impractical in every way, for it is hot and noisy and disintegrates far more quickly than thatch.

There are temples in other bandjars of Sangsit which deserve mention. One has an unusual triple gateway leading to the inner courtyard. It is obviously a ceremonial gateway, for it has five steps leading up to the entrance which, however, is of the tjandi bentar, or split, type, whereas the gates on either side have circular heads. It is high and narrow and rather delicate in design, and is constructed of brick, with ornamentation of paras. The decoration is for the most part leaf designs, but on either side of the central gate there is a lion in high relief, and over each of the two side entrances is an exaggerated Bhoma head with huge mouth and long fangs. Within the second courtyard there are several shrines, and the largest is of particular interest. It is on a platform raised three steps from the ground. At the top of these steps, which completely surround the platform, is a small ceremonial gateway directly in front of the shrine and not more than a few feet from it. The gateway itself has three ascending roofs, quite similar to a meroe, though they are of stone. The roof of the shrine is of tile and the walls are carved in the ordinary floral and foliated designs, but on the upper part there are several rangdas whose wild mien conveys the impression of anger or despair. At each corner of the platform there is an ornamental pillar and about the gateway are gathered four rangdas. One of these rangdas is crouched upon several coiled serpents; each foot is on the head of a serpent, and the head of a third serpent extends upward, the protruding tongue licking at the long red tongue of the rangda herself. The rangda rings a small bell with one hand and curls the other hand about her ear, as though listening.

Another temple at Sangsit stands at the top of a high hill and is notable chiefly for its coloring. The entrance gateway is of the conventional split type with rather conservative ornamentation. The guardian raksasas, however, are painted a gaudy yellow and red, and the gateway is a canary yellow with stripes of brown. The low relief is accentuated with white lines, and the Garoedas and the Bhoma heads on either side of the entrance are touched with lavender and red.

Although color is very common in the temples of North Bali, I have only twice seen it used in the southern part of the island; once at a temple on the beach at Sanoer and again in a temple near Padang. In both of these instances, the color was applied only to sculptured figures and not to the temple itself. There are several interesting pieces of sculpture in the temple at Sangsit; one, a gnome riding a dragon, recalls the illustrations in books of European fairy tales, but the gnome is ringing a bell of the same type used by high priests in Bali and the dragon has many of the characteristics of a naga. There are also sculptures of princes, several fierce Bhoma heads, and four seated lions who balance on their heads the pillars which support the roof of a shrine.

The sculptured figures of animals very often form pedestals for pillars in Bali, and in many of the old temples there are beautifully carved figures on the tie-beams which support king posts that rise to the roof.

There is a magnificent temple at Koeboetambahan. The entrance is protected by three ascending terraces, each with dozens of raksasas armed with clubs. There are three split gateways decorated in a bold floral design, rising on successively higher terraces to a central shrine which culminates in a tall spire, framed in turn by each gateway with its guardian raksasas on either side. The protective screen usually found behind the ceremonial gateway is in front of the entrance. There are some notable bits of sculpture and some fine carved and gilded doors in this temple, and the floral design is carried to the point where a huge flower becomes the wheel of a bicycle ridden by a Balinese man.

Such fanciful ideas are common to the North Bali temples, and it is not surprising to find a sculptured Dutchman kissing a girl in the temple at Soewoeg, or a series of reliefs at Moendoek of Dutchmen eating and drinking. At Djagaraga there is a scene depicting several raksasas in an automobile being held up by a highwayman with a pistol. But perhaps the most fanciful reliefs of all are at Menjali, where in one phrenetic panel a Dutchman rides a bicycle, another falls out of an airplane which is being pursued by a second plane, and a third fishes in a sea of huge fish, while Balinese children fly kites.

In spite of the spectacular nature of the large temples, Balinese life centers about the house temple, the small village temple, and the temple in the fields, on the mountains, or by the sea. There are tiny shrines sometimes entirely enveloped by the roots of huge banyan trees. There are others nestling at the foot of forest giants, and close to the river near Batoean there is a shrine resembling a miniature pyramid. Close to Sanoer there is another tiny shrine scarcely larger than a bird house. It is ringed about with a low mud wall, and in this small enclosure, not more than ten feet square, there is a single frangipani tree. A lake laps at the walls of the little temple, and palm trees are reflected in the placid water. This is an idyllic spot, in keeping with the simplicity of the everyday life of the people.

These are the simplest temples, but they are never without their offerings. There are others, not much larger, standing amid the growing rice; small square enclosures with walls lichen-tinted a beautiful, warm red; in each corner a gnarled frangipani tree, and, in the middle, the black palm-fiber roofs of a few small shrines. In one such temple near Mambal, a tall bamboo pole stood in one corner of the temple enclosure. It was slotted at intervals, and as the wind blew through it, it gave off an eerie wail. I have seen similar bamboo poles in the mountains close to Kintamani.

There are several very primitive temples on the beach near Sanoer, built of loosely laid pieces of coral. In one, the principal shrine is a small building on top of a huge pyramid of coral, more than fifteen feet high and at least fifteen feet square at the base. In another the entrance is through a massive split gateway much broader than it is high, roughly built of coral and with only a suggestion of ornament at the top where a few stones have been rudely shaped. This gate is guarded by two unusual raksasas, one very heavy and gross, the other with the face of a satyr. In the center of the first courtyard there is a square base and on it the realistic bust of a Balinese woman. Her long hair falls down her back and her lips and eyeballs are painted crimson. In a country where all art is conventionalized, it is surprising to come upon a figure which might have been copied from life, but in this temple all the sculpture is very primitive and free in its conception. Directly behind this bust are three small shrines, the center one containing the large stone head of a man, and in the inner courtyard is another large head in a small shrine. There are yet other strange figures: a raksasa in the guise of a woman, two rude figures with the heads and trunks of elephants, and one very peculiar figure of a woman dressed in a kain and seated in a chair with her mouth open, gazing vacantly into space. It is difficult to understand what the figure may be parodying. All of these figures are painted white and are decorated with blue, red, and black paint.

There are other temples along the coast, such as the one at Seseh, south of Tabanan, which is built on top of a huge rock, isolated from the mainland at high tide. The long swells from the Indian Ocean breaking against the steep sides of the rock send up tall geysers on the calmest days, and during a storm the temple is smothered in a mist of wind-whipped spray. All that can be seen from the shore are the roofs of two meroes and a small shrine.

At Oeloewatoe there is a very holy temple in an extremely isolated spot at the southeastern tip of the peculiar tableland which is connected to the island only by a narrow isthmus. One passes from the rich sawahs of South Bali to an arid and sparsely populated limestone plateau, where some of the finest cattle in Bali are raised. From this plateau, on a clear day, the whole panorama of South Bali is spread before one. The Goenoeng Agoeng rises majestically in the northeast, and a few whisps of smoke indicate the mighty forces still working within the Batoer volcano. The high peaks of Batoekaoeh and Tjatoer are directly to the north, and the mountains of West Bali stretch in a long serrated line which merges into the eastern coast of Java. Sawahs sweep in a gentle slope to the palm-fringed coast line, dark patches of forest clothe the mountain tops, and at one's feet is the small island of Serangan and the artificial causeway leading to the port of Benoa. To the east, Noesa Penida, the island of the demons, is a dark blotch on the water.

Oeloewatoe is reached by an indifferent road which passes through a few poor towns. It is built on a high cliff and one must climb many steps before one reaches a plain gateway.

There are large volcanic blocks inside the temple which partially obstruct the entrance to the inner courtyard, where a low wall encloses several shrines and a meroe. The temple is not at first impressive, but as one approaches the outer wall the full impact of the scene strikes one. Here the Indian Ocean reaches in an unbroken expanse to the polar ice packs, here great cliffs drop on three sides to where the waves break in a smother of white and turquoise foam and recede, exposing pink coral reefs. It is easy to understand why Oeloewatoe is holy, why it is one of the guardian temples of the island. But it is so remote that it is usually deserted. Once a year, at its birthday feast, it is filled with gay throngs of people, but usually only a few small offerings remind one that no temple in Bali is wholly neglected.

At Gadji there is an unusual temple built of cement. The ornamentation on the first gateway, which is of the split type, is very crude, the sides looking like the vertebrae of prehistoric monsters. The entire top of the inner gateway is composed of a huge rangda head with hands raised on either side of the face, the fingers ending in long metallic nails.

At Dendjalan there is a koelkoel tower remarkable for its intricate sculpture and bas-relief. The entire stone base of this tower is covered with the figures of raksasas, nagas, figures from the Wajang Wong, Bhoma heads, and that strange animal, the Gadjamina, which is half elephant and half fish, and is often used for the cremation sarcophagi of people without caste.

There is a broad avenue hewn from the sacred forest at Sangeh. There, at the end of a colonnade of huge trees, their smooth trunks buttressing a leafy roof, is a split gate, still unfinished, and the ascending roofs of a slender meroe. On either side of this avenue is a row of seated figures, their arms and legs crossed, gazing impassively away from the temple and reminding one of the mysterious avenues in the Cambodian jungle. The atmosphere of this temple is of the cool silence of the forest. It is a fitting spot for a hermitage. Only the chattering of the monkeys can be heard. When they are called, they appear from all sides out of the dense foliage and wait eagerly to be fed. There are two bands, each led by a king. These bands do not trespass on each other's section of forest. Thus they live in peace in a typically Balinese manner, each finding their preserve quite sufficient for their needs.

On the coast, south of Gianjar, where the Petanoe River flows into the Straits of Badoeng, there is a temple; a cluster of red tile roofs and arched gateways limned against the distant deep blue slopes of the Goenoeng Agoeng. It is strangely reminiscent of one of the old Spanish missions of Southern California.

At Troenjan, on Lake Batoer, there are gateways which look like balés. They have tall, thatched roofs and on either side of the doorway there are raised platforms with matting where people can sit. These gateways are made entirely of wood and thatch, though the causeway leading to them is of stone.

There is a temple at Sanoer which is decorated with swastikas and a labyrinthine fret similar to that used in Greece.

At Paroeman there is a marvelously designed ceremonial gateway, sculptured on both sides with large, abstract masks. Above the door are three ascending tiers, each with a central niche containing a figure. There are also figures on both sides of each niche. All of the shrines within the temple are on masonry bases, and the columns are supported by sculptured animals: dragons, a grinning tiger on top of a tortoise, elephants, and Chinese lions covered with flowers.

There is no end to this type of decoration. If one roams the island long enough one will find most of the characters of drama and religion, and many others from everyday life, adorning the temples. They are the expression of the daily thoughts of the people, for the Balinese peasant is an extrovert who considers all things fit subjects for temple decoration. A record of Balinese temple reliefs and sculptures would be a reliable guide to the existing state of thought in Bali, and it is unfortunate, from this point of view, that Balinese architecture is so ephemeral.

At one time the radjas and princely families had private temples on which they lavished an unlimited amount of money. These princes naturally had the finest artisans at their service. But after the Dutch reduced their income as well as their rank, they showed an increasing indifference to their own art. The Radja of Karangasem lives in an European residence of lamentably bad taste, and has sold the finest doorways and almost everything else of value from his palace; but there is a magnificent balé in the private temple of the Radja's family at Boekit. In this balé all of the pillars, beams, and rafters are elaborately carved and covered with gold leaf.

The Poengawa of Kesiman tore down his palace to make way for a cement rectangle which could easily pass for a local jail in some Central American republic; yet behind this pseudo-European structure is one of the loveliest temples in Bali. It is entirely surrounded by a moat, and one enters through a tall gate of weathered red brick with purplish overtones. The ascending Bhoma heads above the entrance are encrusted with a soft grey-green lichen, and all of the ornamentation has become rounded and blurred. This gateway is reached by a narrow bridge, and one passes into a fairyland of shrines and balés covered with carved beams and weathered tile roofs. The pale yellow-green water of one lagoon leads to an exquisitely proportioned eleven-story meroe. At its base are seven

Meroe

66 *Temple Gateway at Paroeman*

Temple Gateway at Serangan 67

Rice Barn

Private Temple

70   *Temple at Besakih*

Ceremonial Gateway in Temple at Sangsit   71

72   *Koelkoel Tower*

Offerings in a Temple

74   *Bas-relief*

76   *Modern Wood-carving*

Old Wood-carving 77

Temple Doors

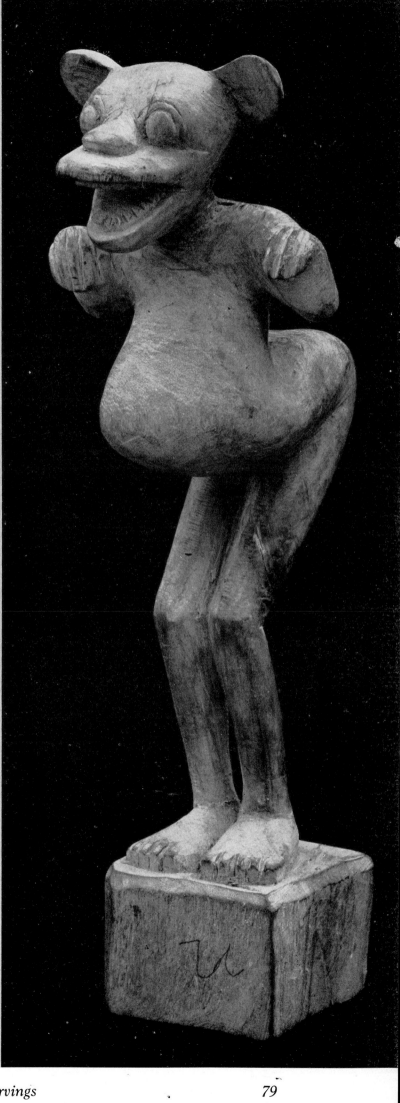

Shrine

kneeling figures. The doors of this meroe are of beautifully carved and gilded wood. All about are exotic plants with vari-colored foliage. Here is exquisite taste, something beautiful and obviously right. Yet the Poengawa tore down his palace, which had been equally beautiful, and substituted for it cement and corrugated iron. He would not destroy the temple, for that would anger the gods, but if it fell into decay, what then? What is this affinity of primitive races for all the claptrap of modern civilization?

The sculptor and the wood-carver in Bali find their widest expression in temple architecture, and this is true in a lesser degree of the painter. But while the sculptor is almost entirely confined by the nature of his medium, the wood-carver and the painter have recently discovered new fields. The wood-carver originally was concerned with the decoration of pillars and temple doors, the carving of figures of animals and gods, and the carving of orchestral instruments, which were given the same lacy ornamentation of leaves and flowers, geometric designs, and demon heads that one sees in the temples. All of this carving was intended to be painted and gilded, but today the wood-carver turns out many clever figures of everyday life—djanger heads, dancing figures, and even exaggerated carvings of insects and animals, all done in exotic native woods. In these modern carvings much is made of the grain of the wood and the figures are given a lustrous, natural finish. Sale of wood carvings by the thousands to tourists has greatly increased the number of carvers, but many fine artists have been seduced by the temptation of quick profits resulting from this mass production.

Many of the old temple ornaments and pedestals for columns are as fanciful as the temple sculpture. I have seen a winged dragon with flames darting from his head and tail, and bunches of hair sprouting from his ears; a winged demon upon a garoeda seated on a pedestal of leering faces; a red dragon with golden wings and huge white fangs curling from his upper and lower jaws, a golden crown upon his head. I have seen whimsical elephants and tigers with black and gold spots upon their hides, and god-carriers cleverly carved to resemble nagas or kneeling bulls. I remember one bull particularly, for he had a most quizzical expression, quite incongruous considering his solemn position. The little gods, one male, the other female, designed to be placed on his back, were carefully stored away except upon special occasions, such as the yearly temple feast. I have also seen a curious charm made to be hung over a child's bed: a winged turtle, its body coiled about by the bodies of two nagas whose heads stuck out of the turtle's back just behind its own head. Behind these naga heads was the figure of a god with a golden headdress. The head of the turtle and those of the two nagas, as well as the turtle's flippers, all moved, and at each gust of wind they dipped and swayed with a fascinating deliberateness.

Temple doorways are often elaborately carved and may be of flower or leaf design in high or low relief, or they may embody the various creatures of Balinese mythology. Occasionally figures from the shadow play are used, and the entire side of a door may be devoted to a single figure; or again, men or animals may be contained within geometric designs, and the remaining space divided between carving and plain areas.

The older Balinese wood-carvings are, almost without exception, painted blue, red, yellow, black, and white, and are finished with gold leaf. The Balinese later learned to mix these colors to form intermediate tones. This limited palette also applied to painting, which until recently was as conventionalized Balinese as wood-carving and sculpture. Its chief characteristic is a confusing, all-over design of foliage, clouds, water, or flame, which fills whatever space is not taken by the characters themselves. Heretofore, painting has probably received less attention than any other of the fine arts in Bali. This is understandable because the Balinese style of architecture leaves no room for mural design, and painting in the temples has been confined to the long strips of cloth which are hung about the eaves of balés on certain occasions. There is no portraiture or easel painting, and the Balinese seldom decorate their homes. The elaborate decoration on the ceiling of the hall of justice at Kloengkoeng is the exception rather than the rule.

During the past few years several European artists have attempted to increase the scope of Balinese painting by providing the artists with new and more flexible materials, and they have been rewarded by some very interesting results. There has been a tendency, however, to ape the style of these Europeans, and it is to be hoped that eventually something more essentially Balinese will develop.

The illustration of lontar books has been carried to a high degree of perfection in Bali. These books are composed of the leaves of the lontar palm cut into strips approximately an inch and a half wide and from a foot to eighteen inches in length. These leaves are held together by a string which passes through a hole in their center, and the covers which protect the top and bottom are made of native wood, of ivory, or of gold. The stories and illustrations, usually from the Ramayana or the Mahabarata, are cut into the palm-leaf with a sharp knife, the tiny grooves later being filled with a black pigment. This work is extremely exacting, and though there are many rough examples of lontar books, there are only one or two artists on the island who can do the delicate work which is so much admired. One of these men, who lives in North Bali, has virtually gone blind because of the severe strain on his eyes, and another in South Bali works only occasionally. In a few years the making of lontar books may have become a lost art.

At one time the working of gold and silver was more common than it is today. The handles of krisses were particularly ornate and were beautifully formed of thin beaten gold with semi-precious stones set in. They usually took the form of a raksasa or a chrysalis. There were also gold rings, gold or silver ear plugs, and the flat bowls of gold and silver which are so often used for carrying offerings to the temple. Now only a few goldsmiths are left at Kloengkoeng; so small is the demand for this type of work that it is rapidly disappearing. This is true also of the richly woven kains and those made of batik, with gold leaf applied over the batik pattern, producing a cloth of great beauty.

Art is so closely bound up with the daily life of the Balinese that it is impossible to mention all of its various manifestations. Yet, they remain an essentially agricultural people. Though a village may specialize in pottery, in silver or gold work, or in woodcarving, its inhabitants still enter into all of the other activities of the normal Balinese life. Specialism, in the sense that we know it, is non-existent.

7

The degree to which a people are adjusted to their environment is the true measure of their happiness.

THE Balinese are the happiest people in the world. They have achieved a remarkable civilization, and live in an almost perfectly equilibrated society; but the conclusions which they have so magnificently worked out and applied to their life, are not applicable to ours.

The civilization of Bali and that of the United States differ in the most basic respects.[1] The Balinese have constructed a communalistic society into which a few democratic principles have been injected, but the first principle of their society is the complete subservience of the individual to the group as a whole. A Balinese judges actions in the terms of ultimate results rather than by the immediate pleasure or pain they may afford him as an individual, for he believes that no matter what happens, the race will survive and that he, too, as an individual, will continue incarnation after incarnation. Call it apathy or what you will, this humility, this effacement of personal pride and ambition, has tremendous power. We, on the other hand, have always stressed individual initiative and individual gain.

The Balinese, moreover, are a homogeneous people who for centuries have known the same environment and physical background, whereas the American people are composed of many racial groups, each striving for recognition at the expense of the other.

The religion of the Balinese binds them together by common ideals, and adat likewise provides a time-tested background of harmonious thought. They are also closely united through the worship of common ancestral gods. In a nation which has more than one

[1] By our society, I mean the society of the United States specifically, and more generally, that of Europe and the Americas.

101

religion there is the ever-present danger that the individual will be torn between the conflicting claims of the various faiths. In Bali this has been avoided, for the Balinese religion is so well adapted to the needs of the people that there is no room for another, and no other could possibly fulfill the same functions. It provides at once the answers to all supernormal and occult manifestations; in short, to everything that the people cannot otherwise understand. But Balinese Hinduism is a colorful spectacle as well as being the answer to the mysteries of nature. It is the focus of all activity; the colorful temple feasts, the dances, the drama, and even the work of these people. Without religion and religious guidance nothing can be done.

The Balinese have been fortunate in that the natural resources of their island have been great, and the population has been small enough in relation to the natural wealth, so that they are a comparatively rich people. This natural wealth has been so well distributed that communalism was possible, and communalism, as it is practiced in Bali, is a highly desirable form of society. The economically independent social groups are small enough so that each person has a definite position and an important function in the life of the community. He therefore enjoys economic security, for all people are inter-dependent. The problems of small groups are greatly simplified, and as each man has a voice in the government, he is close enough to its problems so that he can study them at first hand, and understand them personally. Furthermore, all laws are directly applicable to the people for whom they are made, and all acts of their chosen leaders are obvious at once to the entire community.

The advantages of an agrarian society, quite aside from the problem of economic independence, are clear. The Balinese lead a well-balanced life in which physical labor and sedentary occupations, work and play, are happily combined. They are not exposed to the terrific tensions and nervous strains of so complex a civilization as our own, and are as a result, healthier. Opposed to theirs, our civilization is clumsy and unsatisfactory. Instead of living in one harmonious group in which the problems of government are worked out with proper consideration for all parties concerned, our government must deal with the problems of many millions of persons, and with hundreds of groups, all with different needs. To discover a solution which is equitable is all but impossible. In Bali, restrictions placed upon the individual are seldom onerous. If they tend to become so, they are changed. With us, laws are made for the great masses, and the individual must suffer thereby. It is an anachronism, but it is nonetheless true, that, though our concept of society is that of freedom of the individual, we are much less free in our daily life than are the Balinese.

The dictionaries define civilization as "a state of social culture characterized by relative progress in the arts, sciences, and statecraft.'' Our civilization has attained a very high proficiency in science, and considerably less in statecraft and the arts. The Balinese, on the other hand, have almost no notion of science, and little of statesmanship, except as their own small needs demand, but they are probably the most highly artistic race in the world. Certainly art in Bali finds a greater variety of expression, and a wider application, than in any other country. But, in addition to the fine and applied arts, the Balinese have put supreme emphasis on the art of living. They are almost completely adjusted to their environment, and are therefore almost entirely happy.

Yet the achievements of Balinese civilization have been largely dependent upon the existence of certain special conditions: these conditions are gradually being destroyed, and it seems unlikely that the Balinese can long survive in their present state.

With the conquest of Bali by the Netherlands, the most necessary condition for Balinese existence—isolation—was destroyed. The Dutch have shown common sense and understanding in the policies which they have applied to the Balinese, but their efforts have been able only to stem the tide, not to stop it. The very fact of their conquest has set in action forces which can end only in the destruction of Balinese civilization. Even the most enlightened acts of the Dutch, such as the introduction of foreign medicine, have tended to upset the delicate balance of the Balinese way of life. An increase in population has meant that the same amount of wealth has had to be divided among more people and the per capita wealth has been decreased. The sawahs of many villages have become inadequate, and new land is not always available. In addition to this, the island has been opened to foreign commerce, which has encouraged the importation of European goods, which are coming more and more to supplant Balinese products.

Until recently, the Balinese have always had a favorable trade balance, for they imported nothing, and exported cows, pigs, and copra. Now, though they export no more, they are importing many things: corrugated iron roofs are, in some places, being substituted for thatch; cheap cotton cloth is taking the place of many of the native cloths; bicycles are being bought and European shirts are appearing, as well as gasoline pressure lamps, and other unnecessary innovations. In a few years the Balinese are likely to become pauperized. Dutch schools, taught by Javanese teachers, are breeding discontent by preaching the superiority of the white man and his goods. Young children are being taught to think of their parents as illiterate peasants and of adat as antiquated law no longer of value. The radjas and the princely families have aped the ways of the Dutch, have introduced foreign architecture into their homes, and have, by their example, encouraged the Balinese to wear European clothing. Those Balinese who have become chauffeurs and have had contact with Europeans, the servants in European households, the tourists, and many of the resident foreigners, have all done their part, consciously or unconsciously, to undermine Balinese life. The few understanding Europeans have been in the minority and have been able to do little to counteract the bad effects of others. Tourists have been introduced to the various arts of the island, and the artists now cater to people without experience in Balinese art, who are consequently unable to discriminate between the good and the bad. Although European medicine has been able to decrease infant mortality, the general health of the people has been impaired by the adoption of European shirts and blouses. The missionaries have again taken up their work, and are sowing the seeds of disharmony among the people.

There are still many villages which have scarcely been touched by foreign influence, where life continues as it has for the past five hundred or a thousand years, and there are many Balinese who have never seen a white man, and who care nothing for his civilization. But the time will come when motor roads will extend to the most remote villages, and when the Balinese of the towns will have carried their message of the new culture to every bandjar on the island. The end seems inevitable. It may be hastened by the conquest of Bali by some foreign power whose ideas of government are not so enlightened as those of the Dutch, or it may be many years in coming. Perhaps the war in Europe, with its stoppage of the tourist trade, already has had its effect on remote Bali. Perhaps it has delayed for a year, or even a decade, the fateful day of the final dissolution of Balinese culture.

It is remarkable that such a place as Bali should exist. To have lived there is to have looked at life with other eyes. It is an inspiration to know that man can live at peace and in harmony with man. If it has been done once, it can be done again!

THE END

A NOTE FOR PHOTOGRAPHERS

Photography is the medium par excellence in which to record the living culture of a people. For ten years prior to my trip to Bali I had travelled in most of the countries of the Americas and in Asia. During this time, I did a great deal of photographic work and made wide observations of the customs of the various peoples, but there was always something to interfere with my intention to make a complete photographic record of a country and its inhabitants. At first it was inexperience; later it was lack of time and the impossibility that such a venture would pay for itself. Before I came to Bali I had never discovered any country which had completely captivated my imagination and allayed every desire to look further, but in Bali I knew that I had found a place of such extraordinary interest and unlimited photographic possibilities that many years would be insufficient to capture all of its charm and the magnificent character of its people. I felt that I could spare only one year for the task; nevertheless, here was a challenge, and I determined to remain and to make the most of my limited time.

This book has heretofore dealt with the Balinese people, their dances, their music and their colorful ceremonies; all of which suggest the infinite possibilities for picture-taking. But the photographer will want to know something of the difficulties encountered, the equipment used, and the technique employed. What follows is addressed to him.

The preparation for such an undertaking is equally important to much of the actual work on the spot, and here the photographer can only rely upon his own previous experience or the advice of others. Fortunately, I had had the experience. Simplicity and standardization of equipment are of great importance. Standardization of the cameras used makes it possible for one to become so accustomed to a camera that one's reflexes are automatically adjusted to it, and there is no need for the conscious consideration of mechanical details. A single film size is important, because it is impossible to discover beforehand with which camera one will take the greatest number of pictures. It also simplifies the equipment for developing. Standardization in the type of film used, so far as is possible, is desirable because with a single type of film one can gauge one's exposures more accurately and become more perfectly acquainted with the possibilities and the idiosyncracies of a particular film. It is important to use a single developer for the same reason. One should also select a substantially built camera, a type of film of a standard size that may be bought in a foreign country, should this be necessary, and a developer adapted to the extreme heat of the tropics. Only a few filters are necessary, probably one yellow and one red will be sufficient, and they should be, if possible, of colored glass rather than of gelatin between glass, for in the tropics the Canada balsam is likely to become unstuck, rendering the filter useless.

It is obvious, however, that where so many considerations are involved, some compromises will have to be made. After considerable experiment I have decided on $3\frac{1}{4}$ by $4\frac{1}{4}$ inches as being the film size best suited to my needs. This size is large enough so that with careful development and the selection of a proper emulsion, enlargements up to thirty by forty inches may be made without too much loss of quality. It is also large enough for proper composition on the ground glass and small enough so that a year's supply of film does not increase one's luggage out of all proportion. Cut film is greatly to be preferred over film pack, for the latter has a slight tendency to curl and stick in the tropics, and is, of course, far more expensive. Cut film also comes in a greater variety of emulsions. Used in twelve septum magazines, it is ideal.

Work of so broad a scope as that of recording the entire life of a people must necessarily fall under several categories. There is no such thing as a universal camera, and I have found three to be a minimum. For general scenes, action, and in the case of Bali, the dance, I used a Series D Graflex with a Cook Aviar six inch f4.5 lens. This camera has the virtues of being almost indestructible and of showing a right-side-up image on the ground glass up to the moment that the shutter is snapped. For portraiture in particular, and more generally for distant scenes or action, I used an Auto Graflex with a nine and one-half inch Goertz Dogmar f4.5 lens. This camera has the same virtues as the Series D Graflex, but it has a longer bellows extension. Both of these cameras are used in an identical fashion and so may be interchanged without any switch in one's reactions. They are not, however, suitable to the photography of architecture, for they have neither the necessary movements, nor can lenses of widely different focal lengths be used with them. For architecture I used the Zeiss Juwel A with four different lenses, a Zeiss six inch Tessar f4.5, a four inch Goertz wide-angle Dagor f9, a three inch Goertz wide-angle Dagor f9, and a Zeiss convertible Protar set, ranging in focal length from four and three-quarters inches to fourteen inches. Of these, I have found the Goertz four inch wide-angle lens by far the most useful.

It is essential when doing work of this sort to develop in the field. Only in this way is one able to obtain complete control over exposure and contrast, to check results, and to arrange for the necessary retakes before it is too late. In addition, day to day developing will immediately reveal any defect in the camera. It is naive to think that on a year's trip, nothing will go wrong. While I was in Bali I twice had to take one of my Graflexes completely apart and reassemble it. In selecting developing tanks, it is well to keep in mind that many that are sold are breakable. I have found the Nikor adjustable cut film tank quite satisfactory. Time and temperature development is generally better, but in the tropics, where dark room temperatures range from eighty-five to ninety degrees Farenheit, it is almost a necessity. It is far better to use a slow-working, fine grain developer, adapted to high temperatures, than an ordinary developer cooled with ice, for it is almost impossible to keep the developer, the fixing bath, and the wash water within a safe range in this way. I have found the Eastman DK-20 formula well suited to my work, but it must be used in conjunction with the proper films.

My choice of films was Panatomic-X for all ordinary work and Eastman Superpanchro Press for dance photographs and other fast action. During my stay in Bali I ran out of Superpanchro Press and had to substitute Super-XX, which was entirely satisfactory, though not so fast. Later I imported some Tri-X but was disappointed with the results. It cannot be developed to such a high degree of contrast as the other films, and is unsatisfactory with DK-20 development. The manager of Kodak, Ltd. in Batavia told me that he had not had an opportunity of checking the results of Superpanchro Press film in the tropics. I can report uniformly excellent results, in spite of the fact that some of the film was kept as long as a year, and no attempt made to keep it in a cool spot. All of my film was packed three dozen to a tin, which was soldered, and all film, including the $3\frac{1}{4}$ by $4\frac{1}{4}$ inch Kodachrome, when it was removed from these tins, was immediately put into a water-tight aluminum case, which I used for carrying lenses and cut film magazines. After use, the film was dehydrated in a large tin which was half full of dry rice, and when it was quite dry it was returned to its original tin and retaped. Though Bali is very damp during the rainy season, I had no difficulty with mold. Though there is a very little on a few of my negatives, it does not show up in printing.

At intervals Kodachrome was returned to the United States for development, but black-and-white film was developed never more than a week after it was taken, and the developed films were put into numbered glassine envelopes. Full notes were made during the taking of all pictures and allowance was made in exposure for the type of subject, the intensity of the light, and the effect desired. Development was regulated accordingly. For this reason approximately ninety-five per cent of the more than two thousand negatives can be printed on normal paper. Development was usually carried out at a temperature of from eighty-five to ninety degrees. No sulphate was put into the developer, but a short-stop bath containing potassium chrome alum and sodium sulphate was used. This was the standard Eastman formula for tropical use, and it was followed by the regular Eastman fixing bath. All chemicals, except the sodium sulphate and the potassium chrome alum, were packaged and ready to use after water had been added. It is foolish to attempt to carry solutions in liquid form because of bulk, weight, and the danger of breakage.

This covers the more important aspects of the actual photographic technique involved in such a campaign. It is a matter of trial and error and rigid adherence to rules once made, rather than any genius on the part of the photographer. It is the part of photography which must be learned and then forgotten.

There are certain conditions which the photographer must face in all foreign countries, others which exist in the tropics in general, and yet others which apply to Bali in particular. Language is the first barrier, and in Bali it is a serious one. The ordinary Balinese peasant speaks only Balinese, and there are fewer than a dozen Europeans now living in Bali who understand it. But there are a few Balinese who speak Malay, so in this case I solved the problem by taking with me an European who spoke Malay, and a Balinese who could interpret for him. This rather involved process actually worked out very well, for the fact that I was accompanied by a native inspired confidence in the people of distant villages, and it was possible to secure co-operation which might otherwise have been refused. The Balinese are a naturally friendly race, but in many cases the intrusion of Europeans is resented, and it is only by diplomatic methods that one may finally gain one's point—sometimes weeks later. This brings in the element of time, which is a stumbling block for most foreigners, who are generally accustomed to a great show of speed, even though they don't always accomplish a great deal by it. The life of the peoples of the tropics is geared to a slower tempo than ours, and there is only one way to handle this situation—I have tried them all—that is to suit one's life to theirs. In the tropics one can get things done quickly if one wants to spend a great deal of money, if one wants to get them done in a slap-dash manner, and if one wants to take about ten years off of one's life; but the results are never satisfactory. Bali is no exception, and the vagaries of its religion and the carefree manner of its people, so charming when considered objectively, are nerve-wracking when one is working against time. One must become a philosopher. There is no alternative.

In the morning the photographer will be invited to a special temple feast which is to take place at four that afternoon. At four o'clock he will be there, but he will be the only one. At six o'clock a few people will straggle in. At midnight the feast will be in full swing— very picturesque, but quite useless for photographic purposes. The following morning he will be invited to a dance at four o'clock in the afternoon. At four he will arrive, but unfortunately the people are just leaving. For some reason the dance was held at two. But there are compensations, for very often after being disappointed, he will hear music at a distant bandjar and will happen on something far more spectacular than anything he had planned.

The ideal manner to approach a problem of the sort presented by so complex a race as the Balinese is to spend at least a month without unpacking one's camera. This is a Spartan measure, but the exercise of restraint is well worth-while. Particularly in photographing dances, it is imperative that the dance be seen first. Otherwise one will either hesitate to take excellent shots because of the belief that something more interesting will happen in another moment, or will have used up all of one's film prior to the climax.

There are always problems which arise, both technical and psychological, to tax one's ingenuity. In the mountains there was one town in which I was forbidden to take a photograph. This was not extraordinary, but, in this case, no amount of diplomacy availed. Finally I discovered wherein the difficulty lay. Some half-educated Balinese, who had doubtless been in contact with Europeans in one of the larger towns and had gained a smattering of knowledge, had informed the inhabitants that cameras should be avoided. Why? Because the photograph showed the people naked!

With the correct approach one can gain admission almost anywhere in Bali. The people have an excellent sense of humor and through this, much may be accomplished. One day when I was taking photographs in a rice-field, my assistant stepped off the path and sank up to his knees in the soft mud. The Balinese enjoyed this hugely, so after that we occasionally repeated the performance just to break the ice. Giving an imitation of a tourist taking a photograph is always a sure way to get a laugh; and the enthusiasm shown when I allowed people to look into my Graflex was several times almost fatal to the camera.

The Balinese are quite as willing to laugh at themselves as they are at a foreigner. One day I persuaded a man to pose for me. He was to drink water from a jar, letting it fall into his mouth in a steady stream in the ordinary Balinese fashion. I deliberately delayed snapping the picture while the water gurgled down his throat, and then made several retakes. The man was quite evidently discomfited, but he did not want to be outdone, and kept on drinking until he had drunk almost the full jug of water. His audience was fairly in hysterics, and when he had recovered, he too shared in the laughter.

The Balinese have a naturally graceful posture and a fluidity of line which is innately artistic, but when they are being photographed they usually freeze. Helpful friends who stand about amusing themselves at the model's expense add to the problem, and it is necessary for someone to engage the subject in conversation or otherwise take his mind off of the camera. When dancers and musicians are engaged, crowds always gather, for no matter how busy, the Balinese always have time to watch dancing or listen to music. The natural curiosity of these people makes it very difficult to handle crowds, and people cannot be kept out of the way.

Dance photographs are probably the most difficult of all, and the photographer must have such complete control of his technique that it is second nature and is completely subordinated to the more important aspects of composition and background. When one faces the combined difficulties of focusing on a fast-moving dancer, choosing a suitable background, and composing the picture when it is impossible to anticipate the next movement, there is manifestly little time to consider filters, shutter speed, and diaphragm opening. Add to this that one will want to make both black-and-white and color records, plus a temperature well over one hundred in the sun, plus excessive humidity, plus the fact that somebody will probably step in front of the camera at the crucial moment; and the photographer may decide that the painter has all the best of it. Nonetheless, the camera is unsurpassed in the field of recording action.

For the person who has done much of his work in the studio, the intense one-directional light of the sun in the tropics will appear to be a problem. It was to me. I was sure that all of the shadows would be black and the highlights burned out. After I had worked with sunlight for a short time, I began to appreciate its simplicity, directness, and sincerity. The trickery of multiple lighting was done away with. Actually, highlights and shadows can easily be taken care of by proper exposure and development. Even a reflector is not necessary. A synchronized flash might well be used to advantage, though I did not plan to use one as flash bulbs are bulky and difficult to transport. I had my Mendlesohn Speed Gun with me, but it was not synchronized with any of my equipment, and only once during my stay in Bali did I find it absolutely essential. That was in photographing the Ketjak, a performance in which more than a hundred men, seated in concentric circles, dance and chant. The illumination is apparently from oil flares in the center of the group. This particular case will illustrate how much planning is sometimes necessary before a single picture can be taken. The Ketjak had to be arranged for more than a week in advance and a platform constructed, twenty feet from the ground, between two trees. The camera was lashed to this platform, and as the dance was done at night, it was necessary to focus on a flashlight. This was difficult, as I had to use the Juwel A with the four inch lens, the widest aperture of which was f9. It was desirable to catch the dancers during the actual performance rather than to rely on posing for effect. I finally rigged a thirty foot bamboo pole and pivoted it from the tree on one side of the platform. My flash gun was lashed to the far end of the pole, which was centered directly over the group. The procedure was for two men on the platform to lower the bulb to a point where it was just outside of the camera range. When the proper moment came I opened the shutter, flashed the bulb and closed the shutter. Then the dance would be stopped, the pole lowered, the bulb replaced, and the process repeated. During six hours on the platform, I made less than two dozen photographs. At first, the flash appeared to cause considerable alarm, but later the men seemed to enjoy it, and when I finished I had difficulty in filling the demand for burned-out bulbs.

Walter Spies, an old resident of Bali, tells a story of how he once took a flash picture in the "Bat's Cave," where there is an important temple. As soon as the flash went off, all the bats flew away, and the priest was in great consternation. The bats, it seemed, were the important thing about the place—the holiness had departed with them. Would Mr. Spies be kind enough to pay five thousand guilders, which would buy suitable offerings for the purification of the temple? "Yes, indeed," said Spies, "only I don't have the money with me; I'll come back tomorrow and give it to you." The following day he arrived and, naturally, the bats were back in the cave again. He pointed this out to the priest, who replied, "Well, if you give me fifty cents, I guess that everything will be all right."

The picture of the fisherman throwing his net posed another problem. My intention was to get a fish-eye view of the procedure, and it was therefore necessary to stand in the surf, holding the camera as close to the water as possible, and have the fisherman throw the net so that it landed squarely over my head. In the first place, it was difficult to convince the fisherman that this was what I wanted. I think that he had visions of being charged with assault. When he was finally persuaded, he had to throw the net many times, for often, just when a good throw was made, a large wave came along and the camera had to be snatched out of its way. The next time the action would be wrong, and after each throw I had to be disentangled from the net. This photograph was taken with the Series D Graflex at an aperture of f8 and one three hundred and fiftieth of a second on Superpan Press film.

It is a truism that the photographer has to be willing to do anything and go anywhere. In Bali I walked over miles of trails to reach remote villages. Many of the paths cross streams or skirt the rice-fields. There are no bridges and one has to take one's shoes off and put them on again many times during the day to avoid having continually wet feet.

I finally gave up wearing shoes and thereafter found it easier. Actions of this sort are considered detrimental to white prestige, but as I was quite often taken for a Dutch official, I do not feel that the prestige of the white man suffered too much. I am quite sure that the Balinese were unaware of any breach of etiquette. Several times during dance performances I was in the midst of madly leaping and entranced kris dancers, and one time in North Bali, while photographing the bull races, I found myself backed up against a cactus fence, with two astonished bulls staring me in the face. The photograph, "Bull Racing," was taken at f11 and one one hundred and ninety-fifth of a second on Tri-X film.

Modern emulsions are so well color corrected that I seldom used any filter. "Carrying Coconuts" and "Boats at Serangan" are exceptions and were taken with a red filter. Both were taken on Panatomic-X film with the Series D Graflex, the former requiring an aperture of f6.3 and a speed of one fortieth of a second, and the latter f9 and one fortieth of a second. Whenever possible, architectural studies were stopped down to f64 and averaged about one second with Panatomic-X film.

There is nothing insuperable in the difficulties that the photographer encounters in Bali. Most objections can be overcome with a little diplomacy. The heat will likely affect the photographer's temper far more than the emulsion, but if he will adhere to the laws, respect the customs of the country, and treat the people as his equal, he will have as much co-operation as he desires. Time, patience, and good temper are of the greatest importance. With them, anything can be accomplished.